From th

CW00474265

Welcome to our extra-special new astrological forecast which takes you a up to the end of the century on Decer our year-ahead guides all the astrologic ... be made using tables and a calculator. Today, by the miracle of computers, we have been able to build our knowledge and hard work into a program which calculates the precise astrological aspect for every day in a flash.

When Shakespeare wrote 'The fault, dear Brutus, is not in our stars, but in ourselves', he spoke for every astrologer. In our day-to-day forecasts we cannot hope to be 100% accurate every time, because this would remove the most important influence in your life, which is you! What we can hope to do is to give you a sense of the astrological backdrop to the day, week or month in question, and so prompt you to think a little harder about what is going in your own life, and thus help improve your chances of acting effectively to deal with events and situations.

During the course of a year, there may be one or two readings that are similar in nature. This is not an error, it is simply that the Moon or a planet has repeated a particular pattern. In addition, a planetary pattern that applies to your sign may apply to someone else's sign at some other point during the year. One planetary 'return' that you already know well is the Solar return that occurs every year on your birthday.

If you've read our guides before, you'll know that we're never less than positive and that our advice is unpretentious, down to earth, and rooted in daily experience. If this is the first time you've met us, please regard us not as in any way astrological gurus, but as good friends who wish you nothing but health, prosperity and contentment. Happy 1998-9!

Sasha Fenton is a world-renowned astrologer, palmist and Tarot card reader, with over 80 books published on Astrology, Palmistry, Tarot and other forms of divination. Now living in London, Sasha is a regular broadcaster on radio and television, as well as making frequent contributions to newspapers and magazines around the world, including South Africa and Australia. She is a former President and Secretary of the British Astrological and Psychic Society (BAPS) and Secretary of the Advisory Panel on Astrological Education.

Jonathan Dee is an astrologer, artist and historian based in Wales, and a direct descendant of the great Elizabethan alchemist and wizard Dr John Dee, court astrologer to Queen Elizabeth I. He has written a number of books, including the recently completed *The Chronicles of Ancient Egypt*, and for the last five years has co-written an annual astrological forecast series with Sasha Fenton. A regular broadcaster on television and radio, he has also hosted the Starline show for KQED Talk Radio, New Mexico.

•

YOUR DAY-BY-DAY FORECAST
SEPTEMBER 1998 – DECEMBER 1999

LIBRA

SASHA FENTON • JONATHAN DEE

HALDANE • MASON

Zambezi

DEDICATION
For the memory of Gary Bailey, a new star in heaven.

ACKNOWLEDGEMENTS
With many thanks to our computer wizard, Sean Lovatt.

———————————————————————

This edition published 1998
by Haldane Mason Ltd
59 Chepstow Road
London W2 5BP

ISBN 1-902463-08-0

Designed and produced by Haldane Mason Ltd
Cover illustration by Lo Cole
Edited by Jan Budkowski

Printed in Singapore by Craft Print Pte Ltd

CONTENTS

An Astrological Overview of the 20th Century

Next year the shops will be full of astrology books for the new century and also for the new millennium. In this book, the last of the old century, we take a brief look back to see where the slow-moving outer planets were in each decade and what it meant. Obviously this will be no more than a very brief glance backwards but next year you will be able to see the picture in much more depth when we bring out our own book for the new millennium.

1900 – 1909

The century began with Pluto in Gemini and it was still in Gemini by the end of the decade. Neptune started out in Gemini but moved into cancer in 1901 and ended the decade still in Cancer. Uranus started the century in Sagittarius, moving to Capricorn in 1904 and ending the decade still in Capricorn. Saturn began the century in Sagittarius, moving to Capricorn in January 1900 and then through Aquarius, Pisces and Aries, ending the decade in Aries.

The stars and the decade

In general terms, the planet of upheaval in the dynastic sign of Sagittarius with Saturn also in that sign and Pluto opposing it, all at the very start of the century put the spotlight on dynasties, royalty and empires. As Saturn left for the 'establishment' sign of Capricorn these just about held together but as the decade ended, the power and control that these ancient dynasties had were loosening their grip on the developed world of the time. Queen Victoria died in 1901 and her son, Edward VII was dying by the end of the decade, so in Britain, the Victorian age of certainty was already coming to an end. The Boer War was only just won by Britain in 1902 which brought a shock to this successful colonial country.

Pluto in Gemini brought a transformation in methods of communications. It was as Saturn entered the innovative sign of Aquarius that these took concrete and useful form. Thus it was during this decade that the motor car, telephone, typewriter, gramophone and colour photography came into existence. Air travel began in 1900 with the first Zeppelin airship flight, the first powered aeroplane flight by the Wright brothers in 1904 and Louis Blériot's flight across the English Channel in 1909. Edison demonstrated the Kinetophone, the first machine capable of showing talking moving pictures in

1910. Even the nature of war changed as technologically modern Japan managed to fight off the might of the Russian empire in the war of 1904 - 1905.

The Treaty of Versailles, followed by further treaties of Aix and Trianon served to crush the German nation and therefore sow the seeds of the next war.

1910 – 1919

Pluto opened the decade in Gemini, moving to Cancer in 1913. Neptune travelled from Cancer to Leo in September 1914 while Uranus moved out of Capricorn, through Aquarius to end the decade in Pisces. Saturn moved from Aries to Taurus, then to Gemini, back into Taurus, then into Gemini again entering Cancer in 1914, then on through Leo and ending the decade in Virgo.

The stars and the decade

Now we see the start of a pattern. Sagittarius may be associated with dynasties but it is the home-loving and patriotic signs of Cancer and Leo that actually seem to be associated with major wars. The desire either to expand a country's domestic horizons or to protect them from the expansion of others is ruled by the maternal sign of Cancer, followed by the paternal one of Leo. Home, family, tradition, safety all seem to be fought over when major planets move through these signs. When future generations learn about the major wars of the 20th century they will probably be lumped together in their minds - despite the 20-year gap between them - just as we lump the Napoleonic wars together, forgetting that there was a nine-year gap between them, and of course, this long stay of Pluto in Cancer covered the whole of this period.

It is interesting to note that Pluto moved into Cancer in July 1913 and Neptune entered Leo on the 23rd of September 1914, just three of weeks after the outbreak of the First World War. Saturn moved into Cancer in April 1914. Pluto is associated with transformation, Neptune with dissolution and Saturn with loss, sadness and sickness. Many people suffered and so many families and dynasties were unexpectedly dissolved at that time, among these, the Romanov Czar and his family and the kings of Portugal, Hungary, Italy and Germany and the Manchu dynasty of China. America (born on the 4th of July, 1776 and therefore a Cancerian country) was thrust into prominence as a major economic and social power after this war. Russia experienced the Bolshevik revolution during it. As Saturn moved into Virgo (the sign that is associated with health) at the end of this decade, a world-wide plague of influenza killed 20 million people, far more than had died during the course of the war itself.

1920 – 1929

The roaring 20s began and ended with Pluto in Cancer. Neptune moved from Leo to Virgo at the end of this decade and Uranus moved from Pisces to Aries in 1927. Saturn travelled from Virgo, through Libra, Scorpio, Sagittarius and then backwards and forwards between Sagittarius and Capricorn, ending up in Capricorn at the end of 1929.

The stars and the decade

Pluto's long transformative reign in Cancer made life hard for men during this time. Cancer is the most female of all the signs, being associated with nurturing and motherhood. Many men were sick in mind and body as a result of the war and women began to take proper jobs for the first time. Family planning and better living conditions brought improvements in life for ordinary people and in the developed world there was a major boom in house building as well as in improved road and rail commuter systems. The time of lords and ladies was passing and ordinary people were demanding better conditions. Strikes and unrest were common, especially in Germany. As the decade ended, the situation both domestically and in the foreign policies of the developed countries began to look up. Even the underdeveloped countries began to modernize a little. Shortly before the middle of this decade, all the politicians who might have prevented the rise of Hitler and the Nazi party died and then came the stock market crash of 1929. The probable astrological sequence that set this train of circumstances off was the run up to the opposition of Saturn in Capricorn to Pluto in Cancer which took place in 1931. The effects of such major planetary events are often felt while the planets are closing into a conjunction or opposition etc., rather than just at the time of their exactitude.

On a brighter note great strides were made in the worlds of art, music and film and ordinary people could enjoy more entertainment than ever before, in 1929 the first colour television was demonstrated and in 1928 Alexander Fleming announced his discovery of penicillin. At the very start of the decade prohibition passed into US Federal law, ushering in the age of organized crime and as a spin-off a great increase in drinking in that country and later on, all those wonderful gangster films. The same year, the partition of Ireland took place bringing more conflict and this time on a very long-term basis.

1930 – 1939

The 1930s should have been better than the 1920s but they were not. Pluto remained in Cancer until 1937, Neptune remained in Virgo throughout the decade, Uranus entered Taurus in 1934 and Saturn moved from Capricorn through Aquarius, Pisces then back and forth between Aries and Pisces, ending the decade in Taurus.

The stars and the decade

Neptune's voyage through Virgo did help in the field of advances in medicine and in public health. Pluto continued to make life hard for men and then by extension for families, while in the 'motherhood' sign of Cancer. While Saturn was in the governmental signs of Capricorn and Aquarius, democracy ceased to exist anywhere in the world. In the UK a coalition government was in power for most of the decade while in the USA, Franklin Delano Roosevelt ruled as a kind of benign emperor for almost three terms of office, temporarily dismantling much of that country's democratic machinery while he did so. Governments in Russia, Germany, Italy, Spain and Japan moved to dictatorships or dictatorial types of government with all the resultant tyranny, while France, Britain and even the USA floundered for much of the time. China was ruled by warring factions. However, there was an upsurge of popular entertainment at this time, especially through the mediums of film, music and radio probably due to the advent of adventurous, inventive Uranus into the music and entertainment sign of Taurus in 1934.

1940 – 1949

War years once again. Pluto remained in the 'paternal' sign of Leo throughout this decade, bringing tyranny and control of the masses in all the developed countries and also much of the Third World. Neptune entered Libra in 1942, Uranus moved from Taurus to Gemini in 1941, then to Cancer in 1948. Saturn began the decade in Taurus, moved to Gemini, Cancer, Leo and finally Virgo during this decade. The 'home and country' signs of Cancer and Leo were once more thrust into the limelight in a war context. Neptune is not a particularly warlike planet and Libra is normally a peaceable sign but Libra does rule open enemies as well as peace and harmony.

The stars and the decade

To continue looking for the moment at the planet Neptune, astrologers don't take its dangerous side seriously enough. Neptune can use the sea in a particularly destructive manner when it wants to with tidal waves, disasters at sea and so on, so it is interesting to note that the war in the West was almost lost for the allies at sea due to the success of the German U-boats. Hitler gambled on a quick end to the war in the east and shut his mind to Napoleon's experience of the Russian winter. Saturn through Cancer and Leo, followed by the inventive sign of Uranus entering Cancer at the end of the decade almost brought home, family, tradition and the world itself to an end with the explosions of the first atomic bombs.

However, towards the end of this decade, it became clear that democracy, the rights of ordinary people and a better lifestyle for everybody were a better answer than trying to find 'lebensraum' by pinching one's neighbour's land and enslaving its population. Saturn's entry into Virgo brought great advances in medicine and the plagues and diseases of the past began to diminish throughout the world. Pluto in Leo transformed the power structures of every country and brought such ideas as universal education, better housing and social security systems - at least in the developed world.

1950 – 1959

Pluto still dipped in and out of Leo until it finally left for Virgo in 1957. Neptune finally left Libra for Scorpio in 1955, Uranus sat on that dangerous and warlike cusp of Cancer and Leo, while Saturn moved swiftly through Virgo, Libra, Scorpio, Sagittarius and then into Capricorn.

The stars and the decade

The confrontations between dictators and between dictatorships and democracy continued during this time with the emphasis shifting to the conflict between communism and capitalism. The Korean war started the decade and the communist take-over in China ended it. Military alertness was reflected in the UK by the two years of national service that young men were obliged to perform throughout the decade. Rationing, shortages of food, fuel and consumer goods remained in place for half the decade, but by the end of it, the world was becoming a very different place. With American money, Germany and Japan were slowly rebuilt, communism did at least bring a measure of stability in China and the Soviet Union, although its pervasive power brought fear and peculiar witch hunts in the United States. In Europe and the USA the lives of ordinary people improved beyond belief.

Pluto in Virgo brought plenty of work for the masses and for ordinary people, poverty began to recede for the first time in history. Better homes, labour-saving devices and the vast amount of popular entertainment in the cinema, the arts, popular music and television at long last brought fun into the lives of most ordinary folk. In Britain and the Commonwealth, in June 1953, the coronation of the new Queen ushered in a far more optimistic age while her Empire dissolved around her.

L I B R A

1960 - 1969

This is the decade that today's middle-aged folk look back on with fond memories, yet it was not always as safe as we like to think. Pluto remained in Virgo throughout the decade bringing work and better health to many people. Neptune remained in Scorpio throughout this time, while Uranus traversed back and forth between Leo and Virgo, then from Virgo to Libra, ending the decade in Libra. Saturn hovered around the cusp of Taurus and Gemini until the middle of the decade and then on through Gemini and Cancer, spending time around the Cancer/Leo cusp and then on through Leo to rest once again on the Leo/Virgo cusp.

The stars and the decade

The Cancer/Leo threats of atomic war were very real in the early 1960s, with the Cuban missile crisis bringing America and the Soviet Union to the point of war. The Berlin wall went up. President Kennedy's assassination in November 1963 shocked the world and the atmosphere of secrets, spies and mistrust abounded in Europe, the USA and in the Soviet Union. One of the better manifestations of this time of cold war, CIA dirty tricks and spies was the plethora of wonderful spy films and television programmes of the early 60s. Another was the sheer fun of the Profumo affair!

The late 1960s brought the start of a very different atmosphere. The Vietnam War began to be challenged by the teenagers whose job it was to die in it and the might of America was severely challenged by these tiny Vietcong soldiers in black pyjamas and sandals. The wave of materialism of the 1950s was less attractive to the flower-power generation of the late 60s. The revolutionary planet Uranus in balanced Libra brought the protest movement into being and an eventual end to racial segregation in the USA. Equality between the sexes was beginning to be considered. The troubles of Northern Ireland began at the end of this decade.

In 1969, Neil Armstrong stepped out onto the surface of the Moon, thereby marking the start of a very different age, the New Age, the Age of Aquarius.

1970 - 1979

Pluto began the decade around the Virgo/Libra cusp, settling in Libra in 1972 and remaining there for the rest of the decade. Neptune started the decade by moving back and forth between Scorpio and Sagittarius and residing in Sagittarius for the rest of the decade. Uranus hovered between Libra and Scorpio until 1975 and then travelled through Scorpio until the end of the decade while Saturn moved from Taurus to Gemini, then hung around the Cancer/Leo cusp and finally moved into Virgo.

The stars and the decade

The planets in or around that dangerous Cancer/Leo cusp and the continuing Libran emphasis brought more danger from total war as America struggled with Vietnam and the cold war. However, the influence of Virgo brought work, an easier life and more hope than ever to ordinary people in the First World. Uranus in Libra brought different kinds of love partnerships into public eye as fewer people bothered to marry. Divorce became easier and homosexuality became legal. With Uranus opening the doors to secretive Scorpio, spies such as Burgess, Maclean, Philby, Lonsdale and Penkowski began to come in from the cold. President Nixon was nicely caught out at Watergate, ushering in a time of more openness in governments everywhere.

If you are reading this book, you may be doing so because you are keen to know about yourself and your sign, but you are likely to be quite interested in astrology and perhaps in other esoteric techniques. You can thank the atmosphere of the 1970s for the openness and the lack of fear and superstition which these subjects now enjoy. The first festival of Mind, Body and Spirit took place in 1976 and the British Astrological and Psychic Society was launched in the same year, both of these events being part of the increasing interest in personal awareness and alternative lifestyles.

Neptune in Scorpio brought fuel crises and Saturn through Cancer and Leo brought much of the repression of women to an end, with some emancipation from tax and social anomalies. Tea bags and instant coffee allowed men for the first time to cope with the terrible hardship of making a cuppa!

1980 - 1989

Late in 1983, Pluto popped into the sign of Scorpio, popped out again and re-entered it in 1984. Astrologers of the 60s and 70s feared this planetary situation in case it brought the ultimate Plutonic destruction with it. Instead of this, the Soviet Union and South Africa freed themselves from tyranny and the Berlin Wall came down. The main legacy of Pluto in Scorpio is the Scorpionic association of danger through sex, hence the rise of AIDS. Neptune began the decade in Sagittarius then it travelled back and forth over the Sagittarius/Capricorn cusp, ending the decade in Capricorn. Uranus moved from Scorpio, back and forth over the Scorpio/Sagittarius cusp, then through Sagittarius, ending the decade in Capricorn. Saturn began the decade in Virgo, then hovered around the Virgo/Libra cusp, through Libra, Scorpio and Sagittarius, resting along the Sagittarius/Capricorn cusp, ending the decade in Capricorn.

The stars and the decade

The movement of planets through the dynastic sign of Sagittarius brought doubt and uncertainty to Britain's royal family, while the planets in authoritative Capricorn brought strong government to the UK in the form of Margaret Thatcher. Ordinary people began to seriously question the *status quo* and to attempt to change it. Even in the hidden empire of China, modernization and change began to creep in. Britain went to war again by sending the gunboats to the Falkland Islands to fight off a truly old-fashioned takeover bid by the daft Argentinean dictator, General Galtieri.

Saturn is an earth planet, Neptune rules the sea, while Uranus is associated with the air. None of these planets was in their own element and this may have had something to do with the increasing number of natural and man-made disasters that disrupted the surface of the earth during this decade. The first space shuttle flight took place in 1981 and the remainder of the decade reflected many people's interest in extra-terrestrial life in the form of films and television programmes. ET went home. Black rap music and the casual use of drugs became a normal part of the youth scene. Maybe the movement of escapist Neptune through the 'outer space' sign of Sagittarius had something to do with this.

1990 – 1999

Pluto began the decade in Scorpio, moving in and out of Sagittarius until 1995 remaining there for the rest of the decade. Neptune began the decade in Capricorn, travelling back and forth over the cusp of Aquarius, ending the decade in Aquarius, Uranus moved in and out of Aquarius, remaining there from 1996 onwards. Saturn travelled from Capricorn, through Aquarius, Pisces (and back again), then on through Pisces, Aries, in and out of Taurus, finally ending the decade in Taurus.

The stars and the decade

The Aquarian emphasis has brought advances in science and technology and a time when computers are common even in the depths of darkest Africa. The logic and fairness of Aquarius does seem to have affected many of the peoples of the earth. Pluto in the open sign of Sagittarius brought much governmental secrecy to an end, it will also transform the traditional dynasties of many countries before it leaves them for good. The aftermath of the dreadful and tragic death of Princess Diana in 1997 put a rocket under the creaking 19th-century habits of British royalty.

The final decade began with yet another war – this time the Gulf War – which sent a serious signal to all those who fancy trying their hand at international bullying or the 19th-century tactics of pinching your neighbour's land and resources. Uranus's last fling in Capricorn tore up the earth with volcanoes and earthquakes, and its stay in Aquarius seems to be keeping this pattern going. Saturn in Pisces, opposite the 'health' sign of Virgo is happily bringing new killer viruses into being and encouraging old ones to build up resistance to antibiotics. The bubonic plague is alive and well in tropical countries along with plenty of other plagues that either are, or are becoming resistant to modern medicines. Oddly enough the planetary line-up in 1997 was similar to that of the time of the great plague of London in 1665!

Films, the arts, architecture all showed signs of beginning an exciting period of revolution in 1998. Life became more electronic and computer-based for the younger generation while in the old world, the vast army of the elderly began to struggle with a far less certain world of old-age poverty and strange and frightening innovations. Keeping up to date and learning to adapt is the only way to survive now, even for the old folks.

It is interesting to note that the first event of importance to shock Europe in this century was the morganatic marriage of Franz Ferdinand, the heir to the massively powerful Austro-Hungarian throne. This took place in the summer of 1900. The unpopularity of this controlling and repressive empire fell on its head in Sarajevo on the 28th of July 1914. This mighty empire is now almost forgotten, but its death throes are still being played out in and around Sarajevo today - which only goes to show how long it can take for anything to be settled.

Technically the twentieth century only ends at the beginning of the year 2001 but most of us will be celebrating the end of the century and the end of the millennium and the end of the last day of 1999 - that is if we are all here of course! A famous prediction of global disaster comes from the writings of the French writer, doctor and astrologer Nostradamus (1503–66):

- The year 1999, seventh month,
- From the sky will come a great King of Terror:
- To bring back to life the great King of the Mongols,
- Before and after Mars reigns.
  (Quatrain X:72 from the *Centuries*)

Jonathan has worked out that with the adjustments of the calendar from the time of Nostradamus, the date of the predicted disaster will be the 11th of August 1999. As it happens there will be a total eclipse of the Sun at ten past eleven on that day at 18 degrees of Leo. We have already seen how the signs of Cancer, Leo and Libra seem to be the ones that are most clearly associated with war and this reference to 'Mars reigning' is the fact that Mars is the god of war. Therefore, the prediction suggests that an Oriental king will wage a war from the sky that brings terror to the world. Some people have suggested that this event would bring about the end of the world but that is not what the prediction actually says. A look back over the 1900s has proved this whole century to be one of terror from the skies but it would be awful to think that there would be yet another war, this time emanating from Mongolia. Terrible but not altogether impossible to imagine I guess. Well, let us hope that we are all here for us to write and for you to enjoy the next set of zodiac books for the turn of the millennium and beyond.

2000 onwards: a very brief look forward

The scientific exploration and eventual colonization of space is on the way now. Scorpio rules fossil fuels and there will be no major planets passing through this sign for quite a while so alternative fuel sources will have to be sought. Maybe it will be the entry of Uranus into the pioneering sign of Aries in January 2012 that will make a start on this. The unusual line up of the 'ancient seven' planets of Sun, Moon, Mercury, Venus, Mars and Saturn in Taurus on the 5th of May 2000 will be interesting. Taurus represents such matters as land, farming, building, cooking, flowers, the sensual beauty of music, dancing and the arts. Jonathan and Sasha will work out the astrological possibilities for the future in depth and put out ideas together for you in a future book.

The Essential Libra

YOUR RULING PLANET Venus is your ruling body. Venus was the Roman goddess of love and romance. Venus is also associated with luxury and such activities as eating, drinking and merrymaking.

YOUR SYMBOL Your symbol is the scales. The poet, Manilius, writing in the first century AD said of this sign: 'Day and night are weighed in Libra's scales, Equal a while, at last the night prevails.' This suggests the order of light and darkness. The scales obviously have something to do with weighing and measuring, and also the legal profession. Librans like to weigh up all sides of an argument before making a decision.

PARTS OF THE BODY The soft organs such as the bladder and kidneys. Libra also rules the ability to move and walk, so your sign is also associated with the lower spine.

YOUR GOOD BITS You are pleasant, charming and friendly. You are also fair-minded and a good arbitrator.

YOUR BAD BITS You can be lazy, indecisive and totally unrealistic. You can also be a bully when you want to be!

YOUR WEAKNESSES Love, sex, food, drink, pleasure and luxury.

YOUR BEST DAY Friday. This is traditionally Venus's day.

YOUR WORST DAY Wednesday.

YOUR COLOURS Sky blue, leaf green, pink.

CITIES Lisbon, Nottingham, Antwerp, Vienna, Copenhagen, Frankfurt.

COUNTRIES Austria, Burma (Myanmar), Argentina, Japan, Tibet.

HOLIDAYS You enjoy spending your holidays in luxurious surroundings where you can be sure of good food and excellent service. If there is a chance to flirt with the locals, so much the better! You also love short city breaks.

LIBRA

YOUR FAVOURITE CAR Given half a chance, you definitely go for an auto that you cannot afford, such as a large, fast Jaguar. However, you are more concerned about the appearance of the car and its interiors than the state of the engine!

YOUR FAVOURITE MEAL OUT You enjoy dining out at high-profile, expensive, impressive surroundings with music playing in the background. Many Librans enjoy interesting, novel and very spicy foods. Astrological tradition also suggests the cherry and the pomegranate as Libran favourites.

YOUR FAVOURITE DRINK You enjoy sophisticated drinks such as cocktails and good wines.

YOUR HERBS Mint, aloe.

YOUR TREE The cypress.

YOUR FLOWER The rose.

YOUR ANIMALS Rabbit, small deer, pelican.

YOUR METAL Copper. The colours for Venus are pink and green, and copper is an attractive pinkish metal that turns green when it oxidizes, or rusts. Copper is made from malachite, a wonderfully rich green stone.

YOUR GEMS There are a number of gems associated with your sign including the sapphire, emerald and also jade.

MODE OF DRESS You love looking good and prefer to buy expensive, tasteful, elegant clothes rather than funny or flashy ones.

YOUR CAREERS Lawyer, counsellor, designer, decorator, personnel officer, restaurateur.

YOUR FRIENDS Logical and intelligent people who are also attractive, amusing and successful. You enjoy the company of independent people and those who can take care of you.

YOUR ENEMIES Scruffy or loud and coarse types.

L I B R A

YOUR FAVOURITE GIFT You love beauty and luxury so good clothes, something attractive for the home or nice cosmetics please you. Women would appreciate a day out at a health and beauty spa followed by a visit to a hair salon. Men enjoy good-looking status symbols such as a smart briefcase, desk set or watch. Artistic ornaments and craft items appeal, and you may be a designer-label freak.

YOUR IDEAL HOME You need spacious rooms with music playing in most of them. Elegant, refined decor with chic, decorative ornaments is classic Libran style. You may build an extension for the children and your other relatives, otherwise you are careful about whom you invite to stay.

YOUR FAVOURITE BOOKS You may prefer watching television to reading. However, you do enjoy magazines and newspapers because you like to keep up with what is going on in the world. Picture books appeal.

YOUR FAVOURITE MUSIC You love pop music and melodic music. You may also like certain types of jazz and light classical music.

YOUR GAMES AND SPORTS Golf, aerobics, dancing and even flying light aircraft are popular with you.

YOUR PAST AND FUTURE LIVES There are many theories about past lives and even some about future ones, but we suggest that your immediate past life was ruled by the sign previous to Libra and that your future life will be governed by the sign that follows Libra. Therefore you were Virgo in your previous life and will be Scorpio in the next. If you want to know all about either of these signs, zip straight out to the shops and buy our books on them!

YOUR LUCKY NUMBER Your lucky number is 7. To find your lucky number on a raffle ticket or something similar, first add the numbers together. For example, if one of your lottery numbers is 28, add 2 + 8 to make 10; then add 1 + 0, to give the root number of 1. The number 316 on a raffle ticket works in the same way. Add 3 + 1 + 6 to make 10: then add 1 + 0, making 1. As your lucky number is 7, anything that adds up to this, such as 16, 43 or 124 would do nicely. A selection of lottery numbers should include some of the following: 7, 16, 25, 34 or 43.

Your Sun Sign

Your Sun Sign is determined by your date of birth.
Thus anyone born between 21st March and 20th April is Aries and so
on through the calendar. Your Rising Sign (see page 36)
is determined by the day and time of your birth.

LIBRA

RULED BY VENUS
24th September to 23rd October

Yours is a masculine, air sign whose symbol is the scales. The air element denotes a bright intellect and an up-to-date outlook, while the masculinity suggests a certain toughness, although this may not be outwardly obvious. Your sign is quite contradictory because the dual scales seem to suggest two different kinds of personality, both of which are typically Libran. Some of you are gentle, peace-loving and not particularly ambitious, wanting little more from life than a happy partnership, a pleasant job and enough money to live on without having to worry. If you are this type, you may find it difficult to assert yourself and extremely difficult to make decisions. There is a sub-group of Librans who are so laid-back that they never get anything off the ground, and may exist in a permanent mess, perhaps never really working at a job or keeping a relationship going for long. If you are the other kind of Libran, you are ambitious, determined, energetic, sporty and a bit of a handful. You could be a captain of industry, a great success in a creative field or a go-getting salesperson. The chances are that you are a combination of each of these types, being gentle and unambitious at times and very determined and goal-orientated at others.

Your sign is supposed to be devoted to marriage and there are indeed many happily married Librans. Many of you marry young, stay with the same partner throughout life and thoroughly enjoy it. Some of you get into a relationship when young, split up after a few years and then spend much of your time living happily alone but with plenty of friends to keep you occupied. You can cope with a reasoned discussion, but rows and arguments make you very nervous and unsettled; you really cannot cope with a bad-tempered or hysterical partner. You need peace and quiet and a life where few really difficult demands are made on you. You value your freedom and you resent being restricted by other members of your family.

Those of you who have the stronger, more fiery Libran kind of nature may climb the ladders of industry or politics and you can be a tough and effective negotiator. However, in this as in all other areas of life, you can fall into a habit of seeing things the way you want them to be and taking an unrealistic view. Whatever type you are, you have a bright and agile mind which may be sharply intellectual or highly intuitive. Not all Librans are indecisive, and many can make up their minds when all sides of an argument have been considered, but you do need to take your time. Some of you do not take decisive action because you need to keep your options open. Your fine sense of balance and fair play can lead you to work in the legal profession, to deal with contracts for a living or to act as some kind of agent.

Librans of both sexes are very domesticated and you can happily cope with running a household, even down to doing quite extensive do-it-yourself jobs. Many of you are good cooks. You need pleasant surroundings and you may spend quite a bit of money on electronic gadgetry. A good CD player and a couple of quality televisions are a must. Whether married, living with someone on a permanent basis or as a part-time lover, you are a wonderfully relaxed companion who makes the home a pleasant and comfortable place to be in. You are popular with friends and colleagues because you are pleasant and humorous. However, you do have a temper that can take people by surprise at times, and your pride makes it hard for you to go back to a situation once you have left it. You may mislead a partner by keeping your feelings to yourself or, worse still, by not really knowing what you do feel!

All the Other Sun Signs

A R I E S
21st March to 20th April

Ariens can get anything they want off the ground, but they may land back down again with a bump. Quick to think and to act, Ariens are often intelligent and have little patience with fools. This includes anyone who is slower than themselves.

They are not the tidiest of people and they are impatient with details, except when engaged upon their special subject; then Ariens can fiddle around for hours. They are willing to make huge financial sacrifices for their families and they can put up with relatives living with them as long as this leaves them free to do their own thing. Aries women are decisive and competitive at work but many are disinterested in homemaking. They might consider giving up a relationship if it interfered with their ambitions. Highly sexed and experimental, they are faithful while in love but, if love begins to fade, they start to look around. Ariens may tell themselves that they are only looking for amusement, but they may end up in a fulfilling relationship with someone else's partner. This kind of situation offers the continuity and emotional support which they need with no danger of boredom or entrapment.

Their faults are those of impatience and impetuosity, coupled with a hot temper. They can pick a furious row with a supposed adversary, tear him or her to pieces then walk away from the situation five minutes later, forgetting all about it. Unfortunately, the poor victim can't always shake off the effects of the row in quite the same way. However, Arien cheerfulness, spontaneous generosity and kindness make them the greatest friends to have.

T A U R U S
21st April to 21st May

These people are practical and persevering. Taureans are solid and reliable, regular in habits, sometimes a bit wet behind the ears and stubborn as mules. Their love of money and the comfort it can bring may make them very materialistic in outlook. They are most suited to a practical career which brings with it few surprises and plenty of money. However, they have a strong artistic streak which can be expressed in work, hobbies and interests.

Some Taureans are quick and clever, highly amusing and quite outrageous in appearance, but underneath this crazy exterior is a background of true talent and very hard work. This type may be a touch arrogant. Other Taureans hate to be rushed or hassled, preferring to work quietly and thoroughly at their own pace. They take relationships very seriously and make safe and reliable partners. They may keep their worries to themselves but they are not usually liars or sexually untrustworthy.

Being so very sensual as well as patient, these people make excellent lovers. Their biggest downfall comes later in life when they have a tendency to plonk themselves down in front of the television night after night, tuning out the rest of the world. Another problem with some Taureans is their 'pet hate', which they'll harp on about at any given opportunity. Their virtues are common sense, loyalty, responsibility and a pleasant, non-hostile approach to others. Taureans are much brighter than anyone gives them credit, and it is hard to beat them in an argument because they usually know what they are talking about. If a Taurean is on your side, they make wonderful friends and comfortable and capable colleagues.

GEMINI
22nd May to 21st June

Geminis are often accused of being short on intellect and unable to stick to anyone or anything for long. In a nutshell, great fun at a party but totally unreliable. This is unfair: nobody works harder, is more reliable or capable than Geminis when they put their mind to a task, especially if there is a chance of making large sums of money! Unfortunately, they have a low boredom threshold and they can drift away from something or someone when it no longer interests them. They like to be busy, with plenty of variety in their lives and the opportunity to communicate with others. Their forte lies in the communications industry where they shamelessly pinch ideas and improve on them. Many Geminis are highly ambitious people who won't allow anything or anyone to stand in their way.

They are surprisingly constant in relationships, often marrying for life but, if it doesn't work out, they will walk out and put the experience behind them. Geminis need relationships and if one fails, they will soon start looking for the next. Faithfulness is another story, however, because the famous Gemini curiosity can lead to any number of adventures. Geminis educate their children well while neglecting to see whether they have a clean shirt. The house is full of books, videos, televisions, CDs, newspapers and magazines and there is a phone in every room as well as in the car, the loo and the Gemini lady's handbag.

C A N C E R
22nd June to 23rd July

Cancerians look for security on the one hand and adventure and novelty on the other. They are popular because they really listen to what others are saying. Their own voices are attractive too. They are naturals for sales work and in any kind of advisory capacity. Where their own problems are concerned, they can disappear inside themselves and brood, which makes it hard for others to understand them. Cancerians spend a good deal of time worrying about their families and, even more so, about money. They appear soft but are very hard to influence.

Many Cancerians are small traders and many more work in teaching or the caring professions. They have a feel for history, perhaps collecting historical mementoes, and their memories are excellent. They need to have a home but they love to travel away from it, being happy in the knowledge that it is there waiting for them to come back to. There are a few Cancerians who seem to drift through life and expect other members of their family to keep them.

Romantically, they prefer to be settled and they fear being alone. A marriage would need to be really bad before they consider leaving, and if they do, they soon look for a new partner. These people can be scoundrels in business because they hate parting with money once they have their hands on it. However, their charm and intelligence usually manage to get them out of trouble.

L E O
24th July to 23rd August

Leos can be marvellous company or a complete pain in the neck. Under normal circumstances, they are warm-hearted, generous, sociable and popular but they can be very moody and irritable when under pressure or under the weather. Leos put their heart and soul into whatever they are doing and they can work like demons for a while. However, they cannot keep up the pace for long and they need to get away, zonk out on the sofa and take frequent holidays. These people always appear confident and they look like true winners, but their confidence can suddenly evaporate, leaving them unsure and unhappy with their efforts. They are extremely sensitive to hurt and they cannot take ridicule or even very much teasing.

Leos are proud. They have very high standards in all that they do and most have great integrity and honesty, but there are some who are complete and utter crooks. These people can stand on their dignity and be very snobbish. Their arrogance can become insufferable and they can take their powers of leadership into the realms of bossiness. They are convinced that they should be in charge and they can be very obstinate. Some Leos love the status and lifestyle which proclaims their successes. Many work in glamour professions such as the airline and entertainment industries. Others spend their day communing with computers and other high-tech gadgetry. In loving relationships, they are loyal but only while the magic lasts. If boredom sets in, they often start looking around for fresh fields. They are the most generous and loving of people and they need to play affectionately. Leos are kind, charming and they live life to the full.

VIRGO
24th August to 23rd September

Virgos are highly intelligent, interested in everything and everyone and happy to be busy with many jobs and hobbies. Many have some kind of specialized knowledge and most are good with their hands, but their nit-picking ways can infuriate colleagues. They find it hard to discuss their innermost feelings and this can make them hard to understand. In many ways, they are happier doing something practical than dealing with relationships. Virgos can also overdo the self-sacrificial bit and make themselves martyrs to other people's impractical lifestyles. They are willing to fit in with whatever is going on and can adjust to most things, but they mustn't neglect their own needs.

Although excellent communicators and wonderfully witty conversationalists, Virgos prefer to express their deepest feelings by actions rather than words. Most avoid touching all but very close friends and family members and many find lovey-dovey behaviour embarrassing. They can be very highly sexed and may use this as a way of expressing love. Virgos are criticized a good deal as children and are often made to feel unwelcome in their childhood homes. In turn, they become very critical of others and they can use this in order to wound.

Many Virgos overcome inhibitions by taking up acting, music, cookery or sports. Acting is particularly common to this sign because it allows them to put aside their fears and take on the mantle of someone quite different. They are shy and slow to make friends but when they do accept someone, they are the loyalest, gentlest and kindest of companions. They are great company and have a wonderful sense of humour.

SCORPIO
24th October to 22nd November

Reliable, resourceful and enduring, Scorpios seem to be the strong men and women of the zodiac. But are they really? They can be nasty at times, dishing out what they see as the truth, no matter how unwelcome. Their own feelings are sensitive and they are easily hurt, but they won't show any hurt or weakness in themselves to others. When they are very low or unhappy, this turns inwards, attacking their immune systems and making them ill. However, they have great resilience and they bounce back time and again from the most awful ailments.

Nobody needs to love and be loved more than a Scorpio, but their partners must stand up to them because they will give anyone they don't respect a very hard time indeed. They are the most loyal and honest of companions, both in personal relationships and at work. One reason for this is their hatred of change or uncertainty. Scorpios enjoy being the power behind the throne with someone else occupying the hot seat. This way, they can quietly manipulate everyone, set one against another and get exactly what they want from the situation.

Scorpios' voices are their best feature, often low, well-modulated and cultured and these wonderful voices are used to the full in pleasant persuasion. These people are neither as highly sexed nor as difficult as most astrology books make out, but they do have their passions (even if these are not always for sex itself) and they like to be thought of as sexy. They love to shock and to appear slightly dangerous, but they also make kind-hearted and loyal friends, superb hosts and gentle people who are often very fond of animals. Great people when they are not being cruel, stingy or devious!

SAGITTARIUS
23rd November to 21st December

Sagittarians are great company because they are interested in everything and everyone. Broad-minded and lacking in prejudice, they are fascinated by even the strangest of people. With their optimism and humour, they are often the life and soul of the party, while they are in a good mood. They can become quite down-hearted, crabby and awkward on occasion, but not usually for long. They can be hurtful to others because they cannot resist speaking what they see as the truth, even if it causes embarrassment. However, their tactlessness is usually innocent and they have no desire to hurt.

Sagittarians need an unconventional lifestyle, preferably one which allows them to travel. They cannot be cooped up in a cramped environment and they need to meet new people and to explore a variety of ideas during their day's work. Money is not their god and they will work for a pittance if they feel inspired by the task. Their values are spiritual rather than material. Many are attracted to the spiritual side of life and may be interested in the Church, philosophy, astrology and other New Age subjects. Higher education and legal matters attract them because these subjects expand and explore intellectual boundaries. Long-lived relationships may not appeal because they need to feel free and unfettered, but they can do well with a self-sufficient and independent partner. Despite all this intellectualism and need for freedom, Sagittarians have a deep need to be cuddled and touched and they need to be supported emotionally.

CAPRICORN
22nd December to 20th January

Capricorns are patient, realistic and responsible and they take life seriously. They need security but they may find this difficult to achieve. Many live on a treadmill of work, simply to pay the bills and feed the kids. They will never shun family responsibilities, even caring for distant relatives if this becomes necessary. However, they can play the martyr while doing so. These people hate coarseness, they are easily embarrassed and they hate to annoy anyone. Capricorns believe fervently in keeping the peace in their families. This doesn't mean that they cannot stand up for themselves, indeed they know how to get their own way and they won't be bullied. They are adept at using charm to get around prickly people.

Capricorns are ambitious, hard-working, patient and status-conscious and they will work their way steadily towards the top in any organization. If they run their own businesses, they need a partner with more pizzazz to deal with sales and marketing for them while they keep an eye on the books. Their nit-picking habits can infuriate others and some have a tendency to 'know best' and not to listen. These people work at their hobbies with the same kind of dedication that they put into everything else. They are faithful and reliable in relationships and it takes a great deal to make them stray. If a relationship breaks up, they take a long time to get over it. They may marry very early or delay it until middle age when they are less shy. As an earth sign, Capricorns are highly sexed but they need to be in a relationship where they can relax and gain confidence. Their best attribute is their genuine kindness and their wonderfully dry, witty sense of humour.

AQUARIUS
21st January to 19th February

Clever, friendly, kind and humane, Aquarians are the easiest people to make friends with but probably the hardest to really know. They are often more comfortable with acquaintances than with those who are close to them. Being dutiful, they would never let a member of their family go without their basic requirements, but they can be strangely, even deliberately, blind to their underlying needs and real feelings. They are more comfortable with causes and their idealistic ideas than with the day-to-day routine of family life. Their homes may reflect this lack of interest by being rather messy, although there are other Aquarians who are almost clinically house proud.

Their opinions are formed early in life and are firmly fixed. Being patient with people, they make good teachers and are, themselves, always willing to learn something new. But are they willing to go out and earn a living? Some are, many are not. These people can be extremely eccentric in the way they dress or the way they live. They make a point of being 'different' and they can actually feel very unsettled and uneasy if made to conform, even outwardly. Their restless, sceptical minds mean that they need an alternative kind of lifestyle which stretches them mentally.

In relationships, they are surprisingly constant and faithful and they only stray when they know in their hearts that there is no longer anything to be gained from staying put. Aquarians are often very attached to the first real commitment in their lives and they can even remarry a previously divorced partner. Their sexuality fluctuates, perhaps peaking for some years then pushed aside while something else occupies their energies, then high again. Many Aquarians are extremely highly sexed and very clever and active in bed.

PISCES
20th February to 20th March

This idealistic, dreamy, kind and impractical sign needs a lot of understanding. They have a fractured personality which has so many sides and so many moods that they probably don't even understand themselves. Nobody is more kind, thoughtful and caring, but they have a tendency to drift away from people and responsibilities. When the going gets rough, they get going! Being creative, clever and resourceful, these people can achieve a great deal and really reach the top, but few of them do. Some Pisceans have a self-destruct button which they press before reaching their goal. Others do achieve success and the motivating force behind this essentially spiritual and mystical sign is often money. Many Pisceans feel insecure, most suffer some experience of poverty at some time in their early lives and they grow into adulthood determined that they will never feel that kind of uncertainty again.

Pisceans are at home in any kind of creative or caring career. Many can be found in teaching, nursing and the arts. Some find life hard and are often unhappy; many have to make tremendous sacrifices on behalf of others. This may be a pattern which repeats itself from childhood, where the message is that the Piscean's needs always come last. These people can be stubborn, awkward, selfish and quite nasty when a friendship or relationship goes sour. This is because, despite their basically kind and gentle personality, there is a side which needs to be in charge of any relationship. Pisceans make extremely faithful partners as long as the romance doesn't evaporate and their partners treat them well. Problems occur if they are mistreated or rejected, if they become bored or restless or if their alcohol intake climbs over the danger level. The Piscean lover is a sexual fantasist, so in this sphere of life anything can happen!

You and Yours

What is it like to bring up an Arien child? What kind of father does a Libran make? How does it feel to grow up with a Sagittarian mother? Whatever your own sign is, how do you appear to your parents and how do you behave towards your children?

THE LIBRA FATHER
Libran men mean well, but they may not actually perform that well. They have no great desire to be fathers but welcome their children when they come along. They may slide out of the more irksome tasks by having an absorbing job or a series of equally absorbing hobbies which keep them occupied outside the home. These men do better with older children because they can talk to them.

THE LIBRA MOTHER
Libran mothers are pleasant and easy-going but some of them are more interested in their looks, their furnishings and their friends than their children. Others are very loving and kind but a bit too soft, which results in their children disrespecting them or walking all over them in later life. These mothers enjoy talking to their children and encouraging them to succeed.

THE LIBRA CHILD
These children are charming and attractive and they have no difficulty in getting on with people. They make just enough effort to get through school and only do the household jobs they cannot dodge. They may drive their parents mad with their demands for the latest gadget or gimmick. However, their common sense, sense of humour and reasonable attitude makes harsh discipline unnecessary.

THE ARIES FATHER
Arien men take the duties of fatherhood very seriously. They read to their children, take them on educational trips and expose them to art and music from an early age. They can push their children too hard or tyrannize the sensitive ones. The Aries father wants his children not only to have what he didn't have but also to be what he isn't. He respects those children who are high achievers and who can stand up to him.

THE ARIES MOTHER
Arien women love their children dearly and will make amazing sacrifices for

them, but don't expect them to give up their jobs or their outside interests for motherhood. Competitive herself, this mother wants her children to be the best and she may push them too hard. However, she is kind-hearted, affectionate and not likely to over-discipline them. She treats her offspring as adults and is well loved in return.

THE ARIES CHILD

Arien children are hard to ignore. Lively, noisy and demanding, they try to enjoy every moment of their childhood. Despite this, they lack confidence and need reassurance. Often clever but lacking in self-discipline, they need to be made to attend school each day and to do their homework. Active and competitive, these children excel in sports, dancing or learning to play a pop music instrument.

THE TAURUS FATHER

This man cares deeply for his children and wants the best for them, but doesn't expect the impossible. He may lay the law down and he can be unsympathetic to the attitudes and interests of a new generation. He may frighten young children by shouting at them. Being a responsible parent, he offers a secure family base but he may find it hard to let them go when they want to leave.

THE TAURUS MOTHER

These women make good mothers due to their highly domesticated nature. Some are real earth mothers, baking bread and making wonderful toys and games for their children. Sane and sensible but not highly imaginative, they do best with a child who has ordinary needs and they get confused by those who are 'special' in any way. Taurus mothers are very loving but they use reasonable discipline when necessary.

THE TAURUS CHILD

Taurean children can be surprisingly demanding. Their loud voices and stubborn natures can be irritating. Plump, sturdy and strong, some are shy and retiring, while others can bully weaker children. Artistic, sensual and often musical, these children can lose themselves in creative or beautiful hobbies. They need to be encouraged to share and express love and also to avoid too many sweet foods.

THE GEMINI FATHER

Gemini fathers are fairly laid back in their approach and, while they cope well with fatherhood, they can become bored with home life and try to escape from their duties. Some are so absorbed with work that they hardly see their offspring. At home, Gemini fathers will provide books, educational toys and as much computer equipment as the child can use, and they enjoy a family game of tennis.

THE GEMINI MOTHER

These mothers can be very pushy because they see education as the road to success. They encourage a child to pursue any interest and will sacrifice time and money for this. They usually have a job outside the home and may rely on other people to do some child-minding for them. Their children cannot always count on coming home to a balanced meal, but they can talk to their mothers on any subject.

THE GEMINI CHILD

These children needs a lot of reassurance because they often feel like square pegs in round holes. They either do very well at school and incur the wrath of less able children, or they fail dismally and have to make it up later in life. They learn to read early and some have excellent mechanical ability while others excel at sports. They get bored very easily and they can be extremely irritating.

THE CANCER FATHER

A true family man who will happily embrace even stepchildren as if they were his own. Letting go of the family when they grow up is another matter. Cancerian sulks, moodiness and bouts of childishness can confuse or frighten some children, while his changeable attitude to money can make them unsure of what they should ask for. This father enjoys domesticity and child-rearing and he may be happy to swap roles.

THE CANCER MOTHER

Cancerian women are excellent home makers and cheerful and reasonable mothers, as long as they have a part-time job or an interest outside the house. They instinctively know when a child is unhappy and can deal with it in a manner which is both efficient and loving. These women have a reputation for clinging but most are quite realistic when the time comes for their brood to leave the nest.

THE CANCER CHILD

These children are shy, cautious and slow to grow up. They may achieve little at school, 'disappearing' behind louder and more demanding classmates. They can be worriers who complain about every ache and pain or suffer from imaginary fears. They may take on the mother's role in the family, dictating to their sisters and brothers at times. Gentle and loving but moody and secretive, they need a lot of love and encouragement.

THE LEO FATHER

These men can be wonderful fathers as long as they remember that children are not simply small and rather obstreperous adults. Leo fathers like to be involved with their children and encourage them to do well at school. They happily make sacrifices for their children and they truly want them to have the best, but they can be a bit too strict and they may demand too high a standard.

THE LEO MOTHER

Leo mothers are very caring and responsible but they cannot be satisfied with a life of pure domesticity, and need to combine motherhood with a job. These mothers don't fuss about minor details. They're prepared to put up with a certain amount of noise and disruption, but they can be irritable and they may demand too much of their children.

THE LEO CHILD

These children know almost from the day they are born that they are special. They are usually loved and wanted but they are also aware that a lot is expected from them. Leo children appear outgoing but they are surprisingly sensitive and easily hurt. They only seem to wake up to the need to study a day or so after they leave school, but they find a way to make a success of their lives.

THE VIRGO FATHER

These men may be embarrassed by open declarations of love and affection and find it hard to give cuddles and reassurance to small children. Yet they love their offspring dearly and will go to any lengths to see that they have the best possible education and outside activities. Virgoan men can become wrapped up in their work, forgetting to spend time relaxing and playing with their children.

THE VIRGO MOTHER

Virgoan women try hard to be good mothers because they probably had a poor childhood themselves. They love their children very much and want the best for them but they may be fussy about unnecessary details, such as dirt on the kitchen floor or the state of the children's school books. If they can keep their tensions and longings away from their children, they can be the most kindly and loving parents.

THE VIRGO CHILD

Virgoan children are practical and capable and can do very well at school, but they are not always happy. They don't always fit in and they may have difficulty making friends. They may be shy, modest and sensitive and they can find it hard to live up to their own impossibly high standards. Virgo children don't need harsh discipline, they want approval and will usually respond perfectly well to reasoned argument.

THE SCORPIO FATHER

These fathers can be really awful or absolutely wonderful, and there aren't any half-measures. Good Scorpio men provide love and security because they stick closely to their homes and families and are unlikely to do a disappearing act. Difficult ones can be loud and tyrannical. These proud men want their children to be the best.

THE SCORPIO MOTHER

These mothers are either wonderful or not really maternal at all, although they try to do their best. If they take to child-rearing, they encourage their offspring educationally and in their hobbies. These mothers have no time for whiny or miserable children but they respect outgoing, talented and courageous ones, and can cope with a handful.

THE SCORPIO CHILD

Scorpio children are competitive, self-centred and unwilling to co-operate with brothers, sisters, teachers or anyone else when in an awkward mood. They can be deeply unreadable, living in a world of their own and filled with all kinds of strange angry feelings. At other times, they can be delightfully caring companions. They love animals, sports, children's organizations and group activities.

THE SAGITTARIUS FATHER

Sagittarian fathers will give their children all the education they can stand. They happily provide books, equipment and take their offspring out to see anything interesting. They may not always be available to their offspring, but they make up for it by surprising their families with tickets for sporting events or by bringing home a pet for the children. These men are cheerful and childlike themselves.

THE SAGITTARIUS MOTHER

This mother is kind, easy-going and pleasant. She may be very ordinary with suburban standards or she may be unbelievably eccentric, forcing the family to take up strange diets and filling the house with weird and wonderful people. Some opt out of child-rearing by finding childminders while others take on other people's children and a host of animals in addition to their own.

THE SAGITTARIUS CHILD

Sagittarian children love animals and the outdoor life but they are just as interested in sitting around and watching the telly as the next child. These children have plenty of friends whom they rush out and visit at every opportunity. Happy and optimistic but highly independent, they cannot be pushed in any direction. Many leave home in late their teens in order to travel.

THE CAPRICORN FATHER

These are true family men who cope with housework and child-rearing but they are sometimes too involved in work to spend much time at home. Dutiful and caring, these men are unlikely to run off with a bimbo or to leave their family wanting. However, they can be stuffy or out of touch with the younger generation. They encourage their children to do well and to behave properly.

THE CAPRICORN MOTHER

Capricorn women make good mothers but they may be inclined to fuss. Being ambitious, they want their children to do well and they teach them to respect teachers, youth leaders and so on. These mothers usually find work outside the home in order to supplement the family income. They are very loving but they can be too keen on discipline and the careful management of pocket money.

THE CAPRICORN CHILD

Capricorn children are little adults from the day they are born. They don't need much discipline or encouragement to do well at school. Modest and well behaved, they are almost too good to be true. However, they suffer badly with their nerves and can be prone to ailments such as asthma. They need to be taught to let go, have fun and enjoy their childhood. Some are too selfish or ambitious to make friends.

THE AQUARIAN FATHER

Some Aquarian men have no great desire to be fathers but they make a reasonable job of it when they have to. They cope best when their children are reasonable and intelligent but, if they are not, they tune out and ignore them. Some Aquarians will spend hours inventing games and toys for their children while all of them value education and try to push their children.

THE AQUARIAN MOTHER

Some of these mothers are too busy putting the world to rights to see what is going on in their own family. However, they are kind, reasonable and keen on education. They may be busy outside the house but they often take their children along with them. They are not fussy homemakers, and are happy to have all the neighbourhood kids in the house. They respect a child's dignity.

THE AQUARIAN CHILD

These children may be demanding when very young but they become much more reasonable when at school. They are easily bored and need outside interests. They have many friends and may spend more time in other people's homes than in their own. Very stubborn and determined, they make it quite clear from an early age that they intend to do things their own way. These children suffer from nerves.

THE PISCES FATHER

Piscean men fall into one of two categories. Some are kind and gentle, happy to take their children on outings and to introduce them to art, culture, music or sport. Others are disorganized and unpredictable. The kindly fathers don't always push their children. They encourage their kids to have friends and a pet or two.

THE PISCES MOTHER

Piscean mothers may be lax and absent-minded but they love their children and are usually loved in return. Many are too disorganized to run a perfect household so meals, laundry, etc. can be hit and miss, but their children prosper despite this, although many learn to reverse the mother/child roles. These mothers teach their offspring to appreciate animals and the environment.

THE PISCES CHILD

These sensitive children may find life difficult and they can get lost among stronger, more demanding brothers and sisters. They may drive their parents batty with their dreamy attitude and they can make a fuss over nothing. They need a secure and loving home with parents who shield them from harsh reality while encouraging them to develop their imaginative and psychic abilities.

Your Rising Sign

WHAT IS A RISING SIGN?

Your rising sign is the sign of the zodiac which was climbing up over the eastern horizon the moment you were born. This is not the same as your Sun sign; your Sun sign depends upon your date of birth, but your rising sign depends upon the time of day that you were born, combined with your date and place of birth.

The rising sign modifies your Sun sign character quite considerably, so when you have worked out which is your rising sign, read pages 39–40 to see how it modifies your Sun sign. Then take a deeper look by going back to 'All the Other Sun Signs' on page 21 and read the relevant Sun sign material there to discover more about your ascendant (rising sign) nature.

One final point is that the sign that is opposite your rising sign (or 'ascendant') is known as your 'descendant'. This shows what you want from other people, and it may give a clue as to your choice of friends, colleagues and lovers (see pages 41–3). So once you have found your rising sign and read the character interpretation, check out the character reading for your descendant to see what you are looking for in others.

How to Begin

Read through this section while following the example below. Even if you only have a vague idea of your birth time, you won't find this method difficult; just go for a rough time of birth and then read the Sun sign information for that sign to see if it fits your personality. If you seem to be more like the sign that comes before or after it, then it is likely that you were born a little earlier or later than your assumed time of birth. Don't forget to deduct an hour for summertime births.

1. Look at the illustration top right. You will notice that it has the time of day arranged around the outer circle. It looks a bit like a clock face, but it is different because it shows the whole 24-hour day in two-hour blocks.

2. Write the astrological symbol that represents the Sun (a circle with a dot in the middle) in the segment that corresponds to your time of birth. (If you were born during Daylight Saving or British Summer Time, deduct one hour from your birth time.) Our example shows someone who was born between 2 a.m. and 4 a.m.

3. Now write the name of your sign or the symbol for your sign on the line which is at the end of the block of time that your Sun falls into. Our example shows a person who was born between 2 a.m. and 4 a.m. under the sign of Pisces.

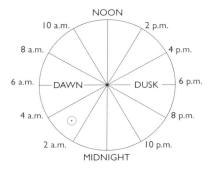

4. Either write in the names of the zodiac signs or use the symbols in their correct order (see the key below) around the chart in an anti-clockwise direction, starting from the line which is at the start of the block of time that your sun falls into.

5. The sign that appears on the left-hand side of the wheel at the 'Dawn' line is your rising sign, or ascendant. The example shows a person born with the Sun in Pisces and with Aquarius rising. Incidentally, the example chart also shows Leo, which falls on the 'Dusk' line, in the descendant. You will always find the ascendant sign on the 'Dawn' line and the descendant sign on the 'Dusk' line.

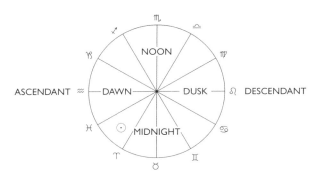

♈	Aries	♋	Cancer	♎	Libra	♑	Capricorn
♉	Taurus	♌	Leo	♏	Scorpio	♒	Aquarius
♊	Gemini	♍	Virgo	♐	Sagittarius	♓	Pisces

Here is another example for you to run through, just to make sure that you have grasped the idea correctly. This example is for a more awkward time of birth, being exactly on the line between two different blocks of time. This example is for a person with a Capricorn Sun sign who was born at 10 a.m.

1. The Sun is placed exactly on the 10 a.m. line.

2. The sign of Capricorn is placed on the 10 a.m. line.

3. All the other signs are placed in astrological order (anti-clockwise) around the chart.

4. This person has the Sun in Capricorn and Pisces rising, and therefore with Virgo on the descendant.

Using the Rising Sign Finder

Please bear in mind that this method is approximate. If you want to be really sure of your rising sign, you should contact an astrologer. However, this system will work with reasonable accuracy wherever you were born, although it would be worth checking out the Sun and ascendant combination in the following pages. You should also read the Sun sign character readings on pages 21–8 for the signs both before and after the rising sign you think is yours. This is especially important for those of you whose ascendant is right at the beginning or the end of the zodiac sign. Rising signs are such an obvious part of one's personality that one quick glance will show you which one belongs to you.

Can Your Rising Sign Tell You More about Your Future?

When it comes to tracking events, the rising sign is equal in importance to the Sun sign. So, if you want a more accurate forecast when reading newspapers or magazines, you should read the horoscope for your rising sign as well as your Sun sign. In the case of books such as this, you should really treat yourself to two: one to correspond with your rising sign, and another for your usual Sun sign, and read both each day!

How Your Rising Sign Modifies Your Sun Sign

LIBRA WITH ARIES RISING This combination brings great potential for success, but you may not be able to finish all that you start due to laziness or impatience over details.

LIBRA WITH TAURUS RISING This is a very artistic combination which also endows you with the ability to cope with details. You love music, cooking or gardening.

LIBRA WITH GEMINI RISING You are an excellent communicator and you may be drawn to legal work or broadcasting. You could be very good-looking, too!

LIBRA WITH CANCER RISING Your family is important to you and you make considerable sacrifices for them. You may work from home or in a restaurant or hotel.

LIBRA WITH LEO RISING You love the worlds of business and glamour and also the good things of life. You could be good-looking and very musical, and you have a great sense of humour.

LIBRA WITH VIRGO RISING This combination makes for a very dynamic personality, but you also enjoy family life. You love cooking, gardening and socializing.

LIBRA WITH LIBRA RISING This is Libra in its purest form. You should be good-looking, rather glamorous and lazy until something comes along to hold your interest. Flirtatious and indecisive, you will be kinder if born before dawn than if born after.

LIBRA WITH SCORPIO RISING You are attracted to politics and you could be very idealistic. You will work for the benefit of humanity, sacrificing your own needs in the meantime.

LIBRA WITH SAGITTARIUS RISING Freedom and fair play is very important to you. You may choose to work in the legal profession, in teaching or in something religious or spiritual.

LIBRA WITH CAPRICORN RISING This strong combination could make you a very successful business person, but you must try to balance this with good family relationships.

LIBRA WITH AQUARIUS RISING You could be very intellectual, with an interest in computers and electronics. Your mind is very active, and you can use your brain-power to help others. However, guard against letting things slide.

LIBRA WITH PISCES RISING You could be keen on fashion, photography or anything artistic or beautiful. You are probably attractive with a dreamy, unworldly appearance.

Libra in Love

YOU NEED:

COMPANIONSHIP A few Librans are loners, but even these have many friends and acquaintances. Most of you are natural relaters who like to have someone in your life. You enjoy talking, listening and discussing life with your partner.

ROMANCE You enjoy it when your lover remembers birthdays and anniversaries and you love to give and to receive little gifts. You love the kind of gestures that keep the romance alive in a relationship, no matter how long you and your lover are together.

SEXUALITY Yours is a particularly sexual and sensual sign and you express your feelings by making love. You enjoy giving pleasure as much as receiving it and you feel reassured when your partner shows you that you are still desirable. You can go without sex if you have to but, if the right person is in your life, you need to feel physically close to them.

YOU GIVE:

CO-OPERATION You encourage your partner to make the most of his or her life, to have a career and to enjoy hobbies, and you try to join in with these as far as possible. You are not obstructive and unhelpful but co-operative and encouraging towards others.

REASONABILITY You are prepared to listen and to understand the views of others, even if they are different from yours. You may be unrealistic at times and you may forget what you agreed to do the previous day, but reasoned argument will always get through to you.

KINDNESS You can be hurtful if you are hurt yourself but you prefer to be kind, and you want your lover to be happy and relaxed. If someone is in trouble, you try to help and you don't criticize others for the sake of it. You are never coarse or crude.

WHAT YOU CAN EXPECT FROM THE OTHER ZODIAC SIGNS:

ARIES *Truth, honesty, playfulness.* You can expect an open and honest relationship with no hidden agendas. Your Arien lover will be a bit childish at times, however.

TAURUS *Security, stability, comfort.* Taureans will stand by you and try to improve your financial position. A Taurean partner will create a beautiful home and garden for you.

GEMINI *Stimulation, encouragement, variety.* Gemini lovers will never bore you; they give encouragement and are always ready for an outing. They give emotional support too.

CANCER *Emotional security, companionship, help.* Cancerians will never leave you stranded at a party or alone when suffering from the flu. They always lend a hand when asked.

LEO *Affection, fun, loyalty.* Leo lovers are very steadfast and they would avenge anyone who hurt one of their family. They enjoy romping and playing affectionate love games.

VIRGO *Clear thinking, kindness, humour.* Virgoans make intelligent and amusing partners. They can be critical but are never unkind. They take their responsibility towards you seriously.

SCORPIO *Truth, passion, loyalty.* Scorpios will take your interests as seriously as they do their own. They will stick by you when the going gets tough and they won't flannel you.

SAGITTARIUS *Honesty, fun, novelty.* Sagittarians will effortlessly keep up with whatever pace you set. They seek the truth and they don't keep their feelings hidden.

CAPRICORN *Companionship, common sense, laughter.* Capricorns enjoy doing things together and they won't leave you in the lurch when the going gets tough. They can make you laugh too.

AQUARIUS *Stimulation, friendship, sexuality.* Aquarians are friends as well as lovers. They are great fun because you never know what they are going to do next, in or out of bed.

PISCES *Sympathy, support, love.* These romantic lovers never let you down. They can take you with them into their personal fantasy world and they are always ready for a laugh.

WHICH SIGN ARE YOU COMPATIBLE WITH?

LIBRA/ARIES
Frequently attracted but it doesn't seem to work for long.

LIBRA/GEMINI
This is a very pleasant and easy-going combination.

LIBRA/TAURUS
Comfortable arrangement both for work and love.

LIBRA/CANCER
Can work but Cancer would probably be too clinging for Libra.

LIBRA/LEO
Extremely passionate partnership
but also massive arguments.

LIBRA/VIRGO
Libran flirtations may get Virgo
down, otherwise all right.

LIBRA/LIBRA
Either excellent or too similar to
spark off each other.

LIBRA/SCORPIO
Scorpio is too possessive for
independent Libra.

LIBRA/SAGITTARIUS
Initial attraction, but it wears off
fairly quickly.

LIBRA/CAPRICORN
Good for business; not so great on
a personal level.

LIBRA/AQUARIUS
Often very successful as neither
seeks to possess the other.

LIBRA/PISCES
Sexy union for a while but both
may tend to drift away.

Your Prospects for 1999

LOVE

This is a make-or-break year for matters of the heart. Many Librans have gone
though split-ups and fresh starts over the past couple of years and this year
looks even more unsettled than ever. This is not to say that the news is bad;
it could be very good indeed but it is not likely to be a quiet or relaxed spell.
Mars in your own sign during January and again from early May to early July
will bring your feelings to the surface and the chances of a passionate
encounter or two at that time are very strong indeed. Even those of you in
very settled relationships will notice that your feelings regarding your lover
are far stronger. The problem is that Mars can cause friction, tension and
arguments as well as passionate and loving moods. Librans can be
argumentative at the best of times and you will have to ensure that you don't
exhaust your partner's patience that you end up arguing your relationship out
of existence. It might be more sensible to give way at times, even though you
know you are right and that your lover is probably wrong. Jupiter opposing
your sign suggests that any partner, whether an old-established one or
someone completely new, would be on a turning point themselves. This
turning point will eventually work out well for the partner himself but
whether this all works in your favour or against you is difficult to assess.

MONEY AND WORK

Both work and money are looking rather good this year and setbacks should be few and far between. Financially speaking, you can expect some real gains from the end of January to mid-March and from early July until early September. However, there could be some losses and setbacks from mid-March to early May. Machinery could suddenly break down at this time, involving long-drawn-out or expensive repairs. If you have any financial dealings with a youngish man at this time, you must watch him carefully and not allow him free rein with your bank account. Partners and lovers will have financial ups and downs this year too and you might be called upon to help them out of a spot, especially from the middle of August onwards. Workwise, the efforts you have put in over the past year or so will pay off handsomely now and you will feel quite happy and confident for once. There might be a slight problem at work during March and April but this time of muddles and problems is not at all severe and you might not even notice it that much. Creative projects will be the most interesting this year and you could find yourself with a real success on your hands by the end of the year. There is such a strong emphasis on children and on youth this year that you might find yourself working with youngsters or for them in some way. You may even give up work for a while in order to have a family of your own to look after.

HEALTH

There shouldn't be much to worry about regarding health this year but you will have to take care during March when colds and chest infections are possible. Also at that time you will have to guard against wrist and hand problems. If you do a lot of typing or keyboard work, try to take a break every half-hour and stop altogether after half a day and do something else instead in order to rest your hands. If you want to get into an exercise regime or to put yourself on a diet for a while, the start of the year is the best time for this. Headaches are possible on occasion this year, especially during May and early June when Mars is badly placed in your sign. Do try to get your eyes tested this year too as you may have some head pains due to eyestrain, especially if you have any close work to do in 1999. Hay fever could also affect your eyes now, so wear sunglasses during the hayfever season, even on days that are not especially sunny. To be honest, apart from these warnings of awkward times, you should be pretty fit throughout this year.

FAMILY AND HOME

The domestic and family scene should be pretty peaceful for you this year. There doesn't seem to be much evidence of major house moves, renovations and decorations but if you do make such changes, they shouldn't cause you much trouble. Older relatives seem to be all right in 1999 and indeed the evidence is that they will have a pretty good year themselves and that their own strength and energy levels will be good. Rather than either making life difficult for you or needing your help, they will actually be in a position to help you if you need them to. Children are likely to be a bit more unsettled than usual this year, especially towards the end of the year.

LUCK

Other people could be very helpful to you this year and even when your own luck seems to run out, you will be able to count on others to help you, possibly in the most unexpected of ways. People whom you have helped out in the past will suddenly repay you in a variety of ways. If you have helped others out financially in times past, they could suddenly pop up and offer to do the same thing for you now.

The Aspects and their Astrological Meanings

CONJUNCT	This shows important events which are usually, but not always, good.
SEXTILE	Good, particularly for work and mental activity.
SQUARE	Difficult, challenging.
TRINE	Great for romance, family life and creativity.
OPPOSITE	Awkward, depressing, challenging.
INTO	This shows when a particular planet enters a new sign of the zodiac, thus setting off a new phase or a new set of circumstances.
DIRECT	When a planet resumes normal direct motion.
RETROGRADE	When a planet apparently begins to go backwards.
VOID	When the Moon makes no aspect to any planet.

September at a Glance

LOVE	❤	❤	
WORK	★		
MONEY	£	£	£
HEALTH	✛	✛	✛
LUCK	☡	☡	☡

TUESDAY, 1ST SEPTEMBER
Moon trine Saturn

You'll be in one of those moods when you could take on the world – and win! There is nothing too complex that you can't handle. No red tape, forms, or documents of any kind will confuse you, and when it comes to money – you're a whiz!

WEDNESDAY, 2ND SEPTEMBER
Void Moon

The term 'void of course' means that neither the Moon nor any of the other planets is making any important aspects today. When this kind of day occurs, the worst thing you can do is to start something new or get anything important off the ground. Do nothing special today except for routine tasks.

THURSDAY, 3RD SEPTEMBER
Moon conjunct Neptune

You'll be looking back to the past today. A wander down memory lane could be triggered by anything from and old memento of happy times to a photograph of someone who is now gone. Know that memories, especially happy ones, are always with you.

FRIDAY, 4TH SEPTEMBER
Mars opposite Uranus

They say that you are stuck with your relatives but you can choose your friends. This is all well and good if you choose good friends, but if you make a bad character judgement this will come to light in times of stress. This, unfortunately, could be just one of those times.

LIBRA

SATURDAY, 5TH SEPTEMBER
Moon opposite Venus

There's an action-packed sky today with the main accent on your life ambitions. You may be dissatisfied with your present career or feel that you aren't getting sufficient financial rewards for your efforts. A friend could point out a course of action that will boost your confidence. Be open to suggestions now, because many opportunities are on offer.

SUNDAY, 6TH SEPTEMBER
Full Moon eclipse

Changes are afoot, especially in your place of work. There may be a sudden and unexpected event or two to face, and you may not be too happy with the outcome. Don't let it get you down!

MONDAY, 7TH SEPTEMBER
Moon sextile Neptune

You'll be in a businesslike mood today. That's not to say that your mind will be on the job, though. Any routine work can be accomplished with ease, but the reason for that is that you'll be thinking happy thoughts and dreaming about the future. There's nothing wrong in this, just as long as your tasks get done.

TUESDAY, 8TH SEPTEMBER
Mercury into Virgo

Mercury enters the quietest area of your Solar horoscope today, so don't expect much to happen in the way of business over the next few weeks or so. You may not feel much like talking for a while and you may want to be alone more than usual because you're feeling off-colour or because you need time to yourself.

WEDNESDAY, 9TH SEPTEMBER
Mercury trine Saturn

If you need to get your point across to those in positions of authority now, you will soon find the right way to approach them. Money matters may appear to be disorganized, but they will sort themselves out in the end.

THURSDAY, 10TH SEPTEMBER
Venus trine Saturn

There's no better time for words of love to be exchanged in private than today… or should we say this evening? The combination of Saturn and Venus may indicate a deepening of emotional commitment and the flowering of long-suppressed passion.

FRIDAY, 11TH SEPTEMBER
Mercury conjunct Venus

Sometimes you find it difficult to show your deepest feelings, but this is not the case today. You may not be able to verbalize your thoughts, but this won't stop you writing them down. You can express yourself clearly now, and may even understand the issues better yourself when you see them in black and white.

SATURDAY, 12TH SEPTEMBER
Moon sextile Mars

You seem to be in a dreamy mood now, but others will want you to be much more active. When you shake yourself out of your reverie you'll enjoy a game of tennis or badminton in the garden with the children or a walk with a friend.

SUNDAY, 13TH SEPTEMBER
Moon square Jupiter

You could be a bit under the weather today, making it hard for you to get through your usual chores. There may be trouble and uncertainty at work and you may feel that you are doing far more than you are being paid for. In short, you are suffering from the classic 'overworked-and-underpaid' syndrome. So what's new?

MONDAY, 14TH SEPTEMBER
Moon sextile Venus

You'll be feeling confident today and, even more importantly, you should feel that your instincts are right. Today's excellent aspect between the Moon and Venus suggests that this is a good time to spend money on items that make you feel good, such as clothes, make-up or hair products.

TUESDAY, 15TH SEPTEMBER
Moon sextile Sun

You deserve a reward for all the hard work you've put in, so treat yourself to something nice. A sense of self-satisfaction is evident today, and it's totally justified. Well done!

WEDNESDAY, 16TH SEPTEMBER
Sun opposite Jupiter

Your mood may dip today as the start of a work project makes you feel anxious. You'll have to call on deep reserves of determination to see it through to the finish. However, the message of the planets today is 'Don't panic'. If you couldn't do the job, you wouldn't have been given the responsibility in the first place!

LIBRA

THURSDAY, 17TH SEPTEMBER
Moon conjunct Mars

The conjunction of the Moon and Mars gives you tremendous energy and enthusiasm for life. Your social life will be particularly action-packed and exciting. However, when it comes to your hopes and wishes, there is no way that events could possibly progress fast enough to suit you as your impatience knows no bounds. With such drive and self-assertion at your disposal, you're sure to make a lasting impression.

FRIDAY, 18TH SEPTEMBER
Moon trine Saturn

You will find subtle ways to manipulate others and sway them to your way of thinking today. If you feel that a particular venture will go well, you are probably right.

SATURDAY, 19TH SEPTEMBER
Mercury opposite Jupiter

It's important to be realistic today. Some news on the job front may cause you to be overly optimistic about your prospects. It's true that an ill wind does no one any good, but are you going to gain from someone else's misfortune? Progress may not be as easy or straightforward as you suppose. Keep your feet on the ground.

SUNDAY, 20TH SEPTEMBER
New Moon

A New Moon in the most psychic area of your chart suggests that the next month will bring you closer to intuitive, psychic and spiritual matters than ever before. You may have prophetic dreams or strange feelings that seem to portend future events. Previously unexplored areas of life may suddenly become important.

MONDAY, 21ST SEPTEMBER
Moon sextile Pluto

There could be good news about a financial matter today. This may not directly concern you or your personal finances but it will have an effect on your pocket. For example, your partner's circumstances may be improving now or the firm you work for may be becoming more profitable, making your job more secure and the outlook rosier.

TUESDAY, 22ND SEPTEMBER
Sun trine Neptune

Your mood is dreamy and possibly somewhat out of touch with reality. This doesn't matter, because there are times when we all need to allow our creative or artistic tendencies to come to the fore rather than concentrate solely on life's more mundane practicalities.

WEDNESDAY, 23RD SEPTEMBER
Sun into Libra

The Sun is moving into your sign now and this will bring a number of goodies along with it. The main event is, of course, your birthday. Birthday time means presents and parties and finding out who your friends are from the kind of birthday cards they send. Otherwise, a quiet day.

THURSDAY, 24TH SEPTEMBER
Mercury into Libra

Mercury moves into your own sign for a while today, and this brings the start of a much more positive phase for you. You need to get down to brass tacks and deal with any outstanding business matters. Over the next three weeks or so you will spend a fair bit of time writing letters, phoning people and travelling around the neighbourhood in order to complete a number of small jobs.

FRIDAY, 25TH SEPTEMBER
Sun conjunct Mercury

You show wisdom beyond your years today. The Sun is in close conjunction with Mercury, ensuring your brain is on top form. Every opinion you express will be clear and relevant to the situation. You could outwit Oscar Wilde just now, since your eloquence is hard to beat. Travel affairs are also well starred.

SATURDAY, 26TH SEPTEMBER
Moon conjunct Pluto

You may see, read or hear something today that changes your life in some small way. Perhaps someone whom you previously trusted and believed in will be caught out by a lie or, alternatively, that someone you hadn't considered to be very important to you before could now start to become a true and trusted confidant.

SUNDAY, 27TH SEPTEMBER
Mercury sextile Pluto

You will be pleased with any news that comes your way now, because it could bring improvement in business and financial matters. You may hear something interesting from brothers, sisters or neighbours today.

LIBRA

MONDAY, 28TH SEPTEMBER
Moon trine Saturn

You are developing an attitude of strength and authority and this will stand you in good stead when dealing with officials or business people of all kinds. People will take you seriously today.

TUESDAY, 29TH SEPTEMBER
Sun sextile Pluto

Although you tend to hate conflict, sometimes a struggle is necessary to crystallize your ideas. There may be an argument today but through it you can learn a lot about presentation and logical debate. We think you'll win this one because you'll have an ace up your sleeve!

WEDNESDAY, 30TH SEPTEMBER
Venus into Libra

There's an upsurge in optimism today as Venus, planet of love, enters your own sign. This should put a much-needed sparkle back into your personality, and you'll find your popularity increases over the coming weeks. You can't fail to charm all around you, for who could resist your smouldering looks and magnetic attraction? Charisma is your middle name from now on, so make the most of it.

October at a Glance

LOVE	❤	❤	❤	❤	❤
WORK	★	★	★	★	
MONEY	£	£	£	£	£
HEALTH	✪				
LUCK	⊌	⊌	⊌	⊌	⊌

THURSDAY, 1ST OCTOBER
Sun trine Uranus

Good news about children and young people will take you by surprise now. You may discover that your children see you as a friend or they may start to act in a more friendly and co-operative manner from now on. Children could be instrumental in introducing you to a new club, society or group of friends.

LIBRA

FRIDAY, 2ND OCTOBER
Moon opposite Mars

Boredom is the enemy today because you're likely to react in an impulsive and even destructive way to anything that holds you back. The fault lies with the Lunar opposition to Mars, which gives you irrepressible energy but limits your outlets. If your hobbies or leisure activities aren't giving you the satisfaction you crave, consider alternative ways to express yourself and regain your enthusiasm.

SATURDAY, 3RD OCTOBER
Moon square Pluto

It may be hard to work out what other people want from you because they aren't behaving in a straightforward manner. The problem may be linked to work colleagues, or it may arise in a social setting. Wherever and whatever it is, guard against believing all that you hear, or allowing yourself to be manipulated by others.

SUNDAY, 4TH OCTOBER
Moon conjunct Jupiter

Today brings great news for job-seekers! If you are looking for a new job or if you're hoping for advancement in your present career, today should bring fortunate news. You should be rewarded for work that you have done in the past, either by a rise in pay or status. Your employers will probably give you a pat on the back and your colleagues should bestow a vote of confidence. We hope so, anyway!

MONDAY, 5TH OCTOBER
Venus sextile Pluto

You may think about re-inventing yourself, because if there are things you don't like about yourself you can now set about changing them. You'll think about your image and may decide to lose weight if necessary, improve your appearance and generally take a more active role in achieving the kind of lifestyle you desire.

TUESDAY, 6TH OCTOBER
Full Moon

Today's Full Moon highlights your personal relationships and urges you to discard anything that's getting in the way of a complete understanding with your partner. In strong relationships this is nothing to be afraid of, yet many will find that a chapter of their lives is about to close. Full Moons show that the past is gone, so don't cling to the old; accept the new in the certainty that the future will be better.

LIBRA

WEDNESDAY, 7TH OCTOBER
Mars into Virgo

Today, Mars moves into an area of your chart that is devoted to retreat and reflection. As Mars is usually such an active planet, this suggests that you are in for a quieter time over the next few weeks. One area of life that might hot up now is that of secrets, so if you want a secret love affair or a secret anything else, now's the time to get it!

THURSDAY, 8TH OCTOBER
Moon sextile Jupiter

We hope that you're good at flattery, because it's a skill you'll have to develop fast today. The Moon contacts Jupiter now so you should be prepared to lay it on with a trowel to get your own way! Fortunately, those you have to impress are all too willing to be swayed. If you want to ask a favour, possibly of a wealthy relative, there won't be a better time to do it.

FRIDAY, 9TH OCTOBER
Moon trine Uranus

There should be a number of pleasant surprises from distant or unexpected sources. You may be invited to join others on a trip overseas or be asked to go to an interesting and unusual event. It is not worth trying to plan your day, because life is likely to be unpredictable!

SATURDAY, 10TH OCTOBER
Mars trine Saturn

Any dealings with men will be easy and successful today. You may have to turn to a man for some specific advice or assistance with a do-it-yourself project. If so, you will get all the help you need.

SUNDAY, 11TH OCTOBER
Neptune direct

The large and distant planet, Neptune, turns to direct motion today, ending a period of muddles and confusion in the domestic and family area of your life. If it has been hard to understand the motives and actions of some of your relatives, then all will now be revealed. Once you know the reason for their strange behaviour it will be much easier to cope with it.

MONDAY, 12TH OCTOBER
Mercury into Scorpio

Mercury's entry into your Solar house of possessions and finance turns your attention to economic realities. If you've overspent for some reason, over the next few weeks you'll devise a practical financial strategy to put your savings back on an even keel. The keen insight that Mercury provides shows that this is a good time to add to your cash resources.

TUESDAY, 13TH OCTOBER
Moon square Mercury

Don't try to plan anything with friends, because even the simplest arrangements will become amazingly complicated. A friend may let you down due to ill-health, and another possibility is that you could be laid low unexpectedly. Take care of your ankles, and don't totter about in the wrong type of footwear.

WEDNESDAY, 14TH OCTOBER
Mercury sextile Mars

You'll be full of enthusiasm today. Dreams you once thought were totally unrealistic will now be seen as achievable. You'll look to the future with renewed confidence and the utter conviction that with a little luck and effort your dreams can come true!

THURSDAY, 15TH OCTOBER
Moon trine Saturn

The aspect between the Moon and Saturn shows that you're in desperate need of some relaxation. Stress levels run high at the moment, but although you've got the stamina to cope you should be kind to yourself, too. Money worries are common under this aspect as are troublesome emotional undercurrents. Give yourself some peace and quiet away from disturbing influences, and the solutions will come to you that much sooner.

FRIDAY, 16TH OCTOBER
Moon square Pluto

Logic seems to conflict with your feelings and intuition today. If you really think that what you're being told is untrue, then take it all with a pinch of salt.

SATURDAY, 17TH OCTOBER
Mercury square Uranus

It will be hard for you to get your act together today. Your ideas are excellent but it may be difficult to communicate them to anyone else. Whatever you try to do today will be plagued by constant interruptions and some fairly unreasonable demands upon your time and attention.

LIBRA

SUNDAY, 18TH OCTOBER
Uranus direct

That strange and unpredictable planet, Uranus, turns to direct motion today, bringing changes in your attitude to love and sex. You may have learned some hard lessons over the last few months, but now a new sense of perspective will make it easier for you to work out what you want and how to get it. If you have had disagreements with children or other young relatives, this planetary movement will help improve communications.

MONDAY, 19TH OCTOBER
Mars square Pluto

There seems to be an underlying and unresolved problem going on in your life now and, although this is not the time to tackle it head-on, it's worth examining it carefully. There may be something going on in the sexual area of your life that makes you feel uncomfortable or unhappy, or other hidden problems which are irking you. This needs thinking about and then possibly discussing.

TUESDAY, 20TH OCTOBER
New Moon

Today's New Moon gives a considerable boost to your self-confidence and personal abilities. You may now feel that a change of image is overdue, so make a resolution to update your wardrobe, have a new hair-do and otherwise alter your appearance to match the exciting and outgoing person you know yourself to be.

WEDNESDAY, 21ST OCTOBER
Moon square Uranus

The planets spell danger for everyone today, so please take extra care when cooking or handling equipment. After you have finished what you are doing at home, at work, in the garden or on the farm, be sure to put everything away safely and to make sure that all fires are properly dowsed.

THURSDAY, 22ND OCTOBER
Sun square Neptune

It's vitally important that you keep your feet firmly on the ground today. You obviously want the best for your family, and a happy, harmonious and luxurious environment. Unfortunately you aren't going to achieve all these laudable aims at once. If you discuss these ambitions with your kin, you'll be in danger of talking at cross-purposes. Don't make any far-reaching decisions now or insist that your plans are adopted, come hell or high water. You'll have changed your mind by tomorrow!

FRIDAY, 23RD OCTOBER
Sun into Scorpio

The entry of the Sun into your financial sector is bound to be good news for your bank balance, and the next month will show a rapid increase in your wealth. To make the best of this Solar opportunity, dust off the account books and take a good look at economic reality. We're sure that there are expenses to cut and investments to make that will generally improve the situation. By the end of this exercise you should find that there's more cash to go around.

SATURDAY, 24TH OCTOBER
Venus into Scorpio

The entry of Venus into its natural home will do your financial fortunes the world of good over the next couple of weeks. This is the start of a profitable time in which money will come to you more easily than in the recent past. The true value of things also becomes an issue now, and you'll realize that quality of life is equally as important as making cash. You'll desire tasteful surroundings and comfort while Venus remains in your house of possessions.

SUNDAY, 25TH OCTOBER
Saturn into Pisces retrograde

Saturn's return visit to your house of health and habits may indicate a period when you will be feeling rather low, or perhaps under the weather due to stress. If the daily routine and work pressures are getting to you, try to do something exciting to cheer yourself up.

MONDAY, 26TH OCTOBER
Sun conjunct Venus

What a great day for co-operating with others. If you need help with a project, you will find just what you are looking for at every turn. Your boss may surprise you by suggesting a rise in salary and you should find that you are valued far more than you realized. This should be a sunny and happy day with much to celebrate.

TUESDAY, 27TH OCTOBER
Moon sextile Mercury

You are getting on so well with your neighbours, colleagues and relatives at the moment that it might be worth inviting them round for a party or a barbecue (weather permitting, of course). Enjoy the happiness that friendship brings.

WEDNESDAY, 28TH OCTOBER
Moon square Sun

Boredom is your big problem today and you'll be tempted to lift your spirits by splashing out on a good night out or the odd treat. Breaking the bank isn't your intent, so don't go mad with the cash card. A demanding child may nag you to provide a toy or fashion item that will appeal for all of five minutes, so don't give in.

THURSDAY, 29TH OCTOBER
Saturn square Neptune

Boring duty calls when you least want to deal with the trials and tribulations of everyday life! You'd rather be far away, indulging your dreams and floating in a sea of romance. Unfortunately, some things are just too pressing to be ignored! Blame it on Saturn, the hard task-master of the zodiac.

FRIDAY, 30TH OCTOBER
Moon sextile Saturn

This is a wonderful day for getting jobs done in and around the home. If you have been feeling guilty about that bit of painting that needs doing, then get it out of the way today while you are in the mood to do it. You may feel like doing the cooking, cleaning, ironing or other certifiably crazy activities.

SATURDAY, 31ST OCTOBER
Moon conjunct Jupiter

This is definitely a day for jollity and self-indulgence. Have fun! Forget the cares of the world and go all out to enjoy yourself. The Moon's conjunction with lucky Jupiter ensures an atmosphere of good humour and optimism.

November at a Glance

LOVE	❤	❤	❤	
WORK	★	★	★	
MONEY	£	£	£	£
HEALTH	✛			
LUCK	♨	♨		

LIBRA

SUNDAY, 1ST NOVEMBER
Mercury into Sagittarius

Mercury enters your Solar house of communications, travel and education from today, so this is the start of a period of chat, information and gossip. Close friends and neighbours may have serious concerns about the environment that you'd be wise to listen to. Of course you have a few salient points to add yourself, so don't be afraid to make your views known. Anything connected to journeys and schooling should go well now.

MONDAY, 2ND NOVEMBER
Void Moon

There are no important planetary aspects today and even the Moon is unaspected. This kind of a day is called a 'void of course' day, because the Moon is void of aspects. The best way to approach such a day is to do what is normal and natural for you without starting anything new or particularly special.

TUESDAY, 3RD NOVEMBER
Moon square Neptune

Your other half could be in a world of his or her own today. You won't make much of an impact on their daydream … no matter what you say. You'll just have to sit it out and wait for this vague phase to pass.

WEDNESDAY, 4TH NOVEMBER
Full Moon

Today's Full Moon gives you an opportunity to shrug off some inhibitions that you learned early on, and haven't quite ditched yet. In sexual matters you could learn a thing or two if you're open-minded. Be prepared to respond to a loved one's overtures in a sympathetic manner – you'll probably enjoy the experience! Apart from your intimate life, the Full Moon helps you put your financial affairs on a firm basis. Unspoken understandings won't wash any more, so make sure that your obligations are fully understood.

THURSDAY, 5TH NOVEMBER
Moon trine Neptune

If you have any kind of joint financial venture on the go, it will start to progress rather well now. A partner or lover's finances will improve and this will have a positive effect on your life and plans. You may, for example, think about making a new home together.

LIBRA

FRIDAY, 6TH NOVEMBER
Mercury conjunct Pluto

Your thoughts will be so deep and complex that you may actually have difficulty explaining yourself; your mind will be like a labyrinth as you navigate the most arcane subjects with ease. You'll have to wait a while before you can explain it to anyone else, though.

SATURDAY, 7TH NOVEMBER
Mars opposite Jupiter

This is not the luckiest of days, so don't take any chances and don't gamble on anything. Keep your money in your pocket and your mouth firmly shut. You may not be able to avoid every form of trouble, but you can at least try to limit it!

SUNDAY, 8TH NOVEMBER
Venus trine Jupiter

There should be great news today in connection with your job and payment for work in particular. You may now receive an excellent offer and this could include a binding document of some kind. Make sure that you read it thoroughly and that you understand it before signing. However, having said this, any offer that comes your way now should be an excellent one.

MONDAY, 9TH NOVEMBER
Venus sextile Mars

You could be surprised to find out just how much someone loves you. You may have been looking at this special man or woman with adoration while, at the same time, wondering if they feel the same way. Today's planets should help put your mind at rest.

TUESDAY, 10TH NOVEMBER
Sun trine Jupiter

You know that you are right and that your thinking is just about spot-on today. Fortunately for you other people also know the truth of what you're saying, and are not about to present any kind of unwelcome arguments.

WEDNESDAY, 11TH NOVEMBER
Moon square Venus

Your feelings are running very high today and it may be hard for you to find equilibrium. A female friend or relative will try to pour oil on troubled waters, but you're swiftly running out of patience. The good news is that others are beginning to sense this and will adapt to your mood. You'll soon get everything back on an even keel.

LIBRA

THURSDAY, 12TH NOVEMBER
Moon square Pluto

There are underlying factors behind a great deal of what is going on around you now, so don't take too much on face value. If someone is trying to antagonize you or pull rank, you'll have to bide your time until you can find the right way to deal with them.

FRIDAY, 13TH NOVEMBER
Jupiter direct

A slow phase that has been affecting your ability to work effectively comes to an end today. From now on you will be able to make progress in a big way, and any efforts that you make now will bring results where they most count. If you are offered a work contract, it should be advantageous to sign it. As with all contracts, take care that you read it through and you understand it.

SATURDAY, 14TH NOVEMBER
Sun sextile Mars

Your mood is bright and breezy and your self-esteem is unusually high. Perhaps the light of love is filling your heart and, if this is being reciprocated, it isn't surprising that you are feeling so good.

SUNDAY, 15TH NOVEMBER
Moon sextile Mercury

Attend to detail today. If you have a tool room or a work box that's in a bit of a muddle, then spend some time tidying it up and restoring order. The same goes for paperwork and bank balances!

MONDAY, 16TH NOVEMBER
Moon opposite Saturn

Other people seem to be landing you with a number of unwanted problems these days because they want you to shoulder their responsibilities rather than deal with them themselves. You may come across a really awkward person, perhaps a 'more than my job's worth' kind of official. Whatever the problem, you will have to put your foot down to prevent yourself from being pushed around or feeling used.

TUESDAY, 17TH NOVEMBER
Venus into Sagittarius

The entry of Venus into your Solar house of communications brings charm and an ability to win your own way by persuasion alone. Someone will find your views very attractive, so a more than passing interest will be awakened by a casual conversation. Short journeys too are going to be fortunate, leading to much needed (and quite painless) life lessons.

WEDNESDAY, 18TH NOVEMBER
Moon trine Jupiter

There's a lot to do today, but you must know that the only way to get everything done is to start. Working out the pros and cons in your head won't do much without some physical effort to go with it. Even boring jobs such as doing the accounts or sorting out a slow-going legal matter can be tackled now.

THURSDAY, 19TH NOVEMBER
New Moon

The New Moon in your house of finance and possessions encourages you to re-evaluate everything you regard as important. You may find that you've been basing your ideas of success on envy, and judging your accomplishments by material things alone. Perhaps you've already achieved a level of security and are now looking for another challenge. Whatever the situation, your future economic fortunes depend on your actions now. Perhaps a visit to a bank manager or financial expert would be a good idea? Improvements in your financial state are not only possible but likely over the next few weeks.

FRIDAY, 20TH NOVEMBER
Mercury square Jupiter

Avoid travelling if you can, because this is likely to be disappointing and frustrating. Business matters that involve travel, anything to do with the export trade or other foreign connections are likely to be a bit muddled today. Murphy's Law will also apply to educational matters, so try to leave travel and education for a more auspicious time.

SATURDAY, 21ST NOVEMBER
Mercury retrograde

When Mercury goes retrograde it has a way of disrupting whatever area of your chart it happens to be in. Unfortunately, the planet is in its natural house of communications, so you can expect missed phone calls, letters that have gone astray and the ever-present 'the cheque's in the post'. It isn't all doom and gloom, however, because you can get things done if you're extra-vigilant. Take more care when travelling and be prepared for delays.

LIBRA

SUNDAY, 22ND NOVEMBER
Sun into Sagittarius

This is the start of a rather busy period. You'll be dealing with correspondence, getting on the telephone and rushing around your neighbourhood at top speed. For the next month or so your days will be filled with activity and you will be buzzing from one job to another like a demented bee. Enjoy the success and the achievement that this brings, but do remember to relax a bit from time to time.

MONDAY, 23RD NOVEMBER
Venus conjunct Pluto

There could be some really great news today in connection with business or money matters. Partners will value your opinions, and those who love you will be happy to support you now.

TUESDAY, 24TH NOVEMBER
Moon sextile Sun

It's a day for simple pleasures and innocent enjoyment. A quiet conversation with a child or younger person should show you that you can still learn a thing or two, and have a laugh as well.

WEDNESDAY, 25TH NOVEMBER
Venus sextile Uranus

Your heart is bursting with love and, wonder of wonders, the object of your desires seems to feel the same way. A friend may act as a go-between in a matter of love.

THURSDAY, 26TH NOVEMBER
Moon sextile Saturn

Today's planets suggest that you should make a gradual start on something new. Whatever you decide to take up now will turn out to be a long-term project, so be sure that this is really what you want for the next few months (or years) before you begin. An older man or someone in a position of authority will be helpful.

FRIDAY, 27TH NOVEMBER
Neptune into Aquarius

Neptune, the planet of artistic excellence, enters your Solar house of talent from today. If you've ever fancied turning your hand to poetry, painting or any other form of creative pursuit, then start now!

LIBRA

SATURDAY, 28TH NOVEMBER
Mars trine Neptune

There are strange and subtle forces working on your behalf today, making it easy to get your own way, especially at home. There may be some extra pressure at work, but life at home will be very productive. This is a great time to get a creative project off the ground or use your artistry for home decoration or refurbishment.

SUNDAY, 29TH NOVEMBER
Sun conjunct Pluto

You are never too old to learn something new! That's the astral message today as the Sun moves into close conjunction with Pluto. You could have a revelation which changes your way of thinking for ever.

MONDAY, 30TH NOVEMBER
Moon conjunct Saturn

It looks as if, at long last, you are beginning to get your relationships right. Although there is still much to be done and nothing will improve overnight, the outlook is much brighter. Any decisions that you take now should have an excellent long-term effect.

December at a Glance

LOVE	❤	❤			
WORK	★	★	★		
MONEY	£	£	£	£	
HEALTH	✚	✚	✚	✚	✚
LUCK	☙	☙	☙		

TUESDAY, 1ST DECEMBER
Mercury sextile Uranus

Pretend it's Valentine's Day and pass on a message of adoration to the one you love! You may even find that eyes meet across a crowded room and love blooms in the most unlikely places. Ah, there's nothing quite like romance!

WEDNESDAY, 2ND DECEMBER
Sun sextile Uranus

If you are waiting to hear from someone you love, then today should be your lucky day. If money or business has been an obstacle to the path of true love, then the news about this is good, too. You may receive a windfall or benefit from a kind of lucky break, and something pleasant but quite unexpected could come your way.

THURSDAY, 3RD DECEMBER
Full Moon

Today's Full Moon concentrates on your higher mind and gives a culturally expansive perspective to your thinking. Anything connected with new learning, higher education and foreign affairs is well starred for the next month. Your intellect will be on top form and you'll have little patience with anything that restricts your movements.

FRIDAY, 4TH DECEMBER
Moon opposite Venus

You and your beloved could having a falling-out today. It may be that you can't agree with each other about your holiday plans, or travel could be the cause of some kind of upset for another reason. For example, one of you may feel that you need to visit your family or take a business trip … just when your other half most wants you to be home.

SATURDAY, 5TH DECEMBER
Mercury sextile Mars

There'll be no point in anyone trying to shut you up today, because the mingled rays of Mars and Mercury ensure that your tongue has a will of its own and your voice could blast through double glazing! At least you'll be interesting, which is more than you can say for some!

SUNDAY, 6TH DECEMBER
Moon trine Jupiter

You're certainly ascending the career ladder these days. A woman will be instrumental in helping you, and there may be a golden financial opportunity in the offing. Don't miss it!

MONDAY, 7TH DECEMBER
Moon sextile Mars

A friend may drop in just when you are struggling to do something tiresome and complicated. This will prove to be a blessing in disguise, because your friend will give a helping hand.

TUESDAY, 8TH DECEMBER
Moon trine Sun

A little of what you fancy does you good, that's the message of the excellent aspect between Moon and Sun today. Your social life will be buzzing with excitement, and there should be many new faces around you. If you've been feeling lonely, this is the perfect time to do something positive about it. Join a club or society and meet people who share your ideals. You'll soon find that you aren't the only person in the world who thinks as you do.

WEDNESDAY, 9TH DECEMBER
Venus trine Saturn

A serious conversation with someone special in your life will renew an understanding. This, in turn, will be expressed as affection. Romance doesn't have to be frivolous as well you know, and even shared worries can bring you closer together.

THURSDAY, 10TH DECEMBER
Moon square Sun

Outwardly you may look confident and successful, but inwardly you may be feeling quite unsure of yourself. Try not to behave in an arrogant or boastful manner in order to disguise it or impress others. Your self-esteem needs a boost, so try to pamper yourself if you can.

FRIDAY, 11TH DECEMBER
Venus into Capricorn

This is a good time to spend in and around your home. You may want to get the garden into shape or possibly do some kind of farming work on your land. The atmosphere around you should be harmonious and happy, and you should feel pleased with your achievements. If you have been at odds with any of your relatives, then kiss and make up today.

SATURDAY, 12TH DECEMBER
Mars sextile Pluto

Your ideas and sense of purpose will be so strong today that you can't fail to get your own way ... even if you do make some enemies in the process. You'll be a forceful and determined soul with some revolutionary concepts.

SUNDAY, 13TH DECEMBER
Moon sextile Sun

A reunion with a brother, sister, or other relative of the same generation will be a marvellous tonic today. You'll get the chance to have a long talk and catch up on all the gossip.

MONDAY, 14TH DECEMBER
Moon sextile Venus

You're about to take the social scene by storm! You're a maestro of dazzling wit and repartee, and your popularity is guaranteed as you eloquently hold forth on any subject under the sun. A lot of laughs and entertaining conversations are on offer now.

TUESDAY, 15TH DECEMBER
Mars trine Uranus

Anything could happen on a day when forceful Mars makes an angle to unconventional Uranus. You'll feel self-indulgent, and why not? Have fun. Do something completely different and blow what anyone else thinks!

WEDNESDAY, 16TH DECEMBER
Moon sextile Neptune

This is the perfect time to make a tasteful purchase for your home. It may be just an ornament or a completely new colour scheme that you have in mind. Either way, you can rest assured that this will be a good thing, improving your mood no end.

THURSDAY, 17TH DECEMBER
Moon sextile Uranus

This is a great day for those of you who are involved with children or young people. If you are a teacher, scout leader or something similar, you will have a lot of fun and success. If you are not involved with youngsters, then be a youngster yourself for once – go bowling, play with your computer or dance around the house to music.

FRIDAY, 18TH DECEMBER
New Moon

The New Moon shows a change in your way of thinking. In many ways you'll know that it's time to move on; perhaps you'll soon find yourself in new company, a new home or among a new circle of friends? Your opinions are likely to change as you become influenced by more stimulating people. Perhaps you'll consider taking up an educational course of some kind.

LIBRA

SATURDAY, 19TH DECEMBER
Sun trine Saturn

No matter how optimistically you view your love life, the Sun's aspect to Saturn shows that there is some work to be done in a close relationship. At least this aspect is positive, so some constructive communication can go a long way to resolving difficulties. A serious talk about your ambitions and ideas will help your partner understand you more.

SUNDAY, 20TH DECEMBER
Moon square Mars

The irritations of those around you won't put you in a good frame of mind if you allow them to get to you. It's all the fault of the Moon and Mars petulantly blowing minor domestic issues out of all proportion. Reasoned argument won't wash just now, since all concerned are determined to fight it out – come what may! You could take out some of the aggression on a neglected household job, and leave the rest of them to battle on.

MONDAY, 21ST DECEMBER
Mercury conjunct Pluto

Anything that pops through your letter box today should bring the kind of news you most want to hear. Negotiations of all kinds will go well now, and it should be easy to turn all situations to your advantage.

TUESDAY, 22ND DECEMBER
Sun into Capricorn

The Sun moves into your Solar area of family and domestic issues for the next month. These spheres of life will now become very important to you. If you have neglected your home or failed to pay enough attention to your family, this is the time to put things right.

WEDNESDAY, 23RD DECEMBER
Mercury sextile Uranus

Today's contact between Mercury and Uranus may be manifested as a sudden and unexpected journey. On the other hand, it could come in the form of a declaration of love from an unexpected source.

THURSDAY, 24TH DECEMBER
Moon square Pluto

It may be Christmas Eve, but you'll go about things with a touch of ruthlessness today. This mood can be beneficial if, for instance, you decide to clear out your wardrobe or work space. You'll toss out all that junk you've been keeping 'just in case'. On the other hand, you could deal ruthlessly with others.

FRIDAY, 25TH DECEMBER
Moon conjunct Jupiter

Healthwise you should be feeling pretty good. Even if you've been suffering from the effects of over-indulgence, the outlook shows that this Christmas there'll be an opportunity to unwind! Connections with foreign countries are also emphasized. If you're looking for work, then broaden your horizons because there's an unexpected opportunity out there, just waiting for you.

SATURDAY, 26TH DECEMBER
Moon square Sun

The path of true love never did run smoothly, and today there seem to be a few spanners in the works. Perhaps your mood is romantic, while your partner's is purely practical.

SUNDAY, 27TH DECEMBER
Moon square Venus

Your partner may bring something home that he or she thinks is absolutely beautiful, but you could hate it on sight. If this is a picture, then hang it somewhere unobtrusive and if it's truly awful, stick it in the back bedroom! Don't make disparaging remarks; this kind of thing isn't worth having an argument over.

MONDAY, 28TH DECEMBER
Mercury sextile Mars

You'll gabbling away nineteen to the dozen today. The planet of communication, Mercury, is energized by Mars, so don't expect to sit still or be silent. Short journeys of all kinds should be pretty eventful now.

TUESDAY, 29TH DECEMBER
Saturn direct

Saturn turns to direct motion in the relationship area of your chart today, and this lightens the atmosphere around you and with your lover. You can now sit down and discuss any differences that have hampered you, and work out a more reasonable and responsible way to deal with it in the future.

WEDNESDAY, 30TH DECEMBER
Moon trine Neptune

If your heart is set on finding love and romance, today's excellent aspect between the Moon and Neptune makes it easy for you to make your dreams come true. If you long to be the life and soul of the party, today should be your turn to shine.

THURSDAY, 31ST DECEMBER
Moon trine Mars

My, you are in a restless mood on the last day of the year! If you can jump on a plane, leave the country and escape to a deserted beach, then do so now! If, like the majority of people, you can only dream of such things, then take a mooch round your local travel agency and see what's on offer for later in the year. Your energy levels are high and you'll be keen to find out what 1999 has to offer.

1999

January at a Glance

LOVE	❤	❤	❤	❤	❤
WORK	★				
MONEY	£	£	£	£	£
HEALTH	✪	✪			
LUCK	♘	♘	♘		

FRIDAY, 1ST JANUARY
Mercury square Jupiter

Leave any travelling alone on New Year's Day if you can, because this is likely to be disappointing and frustrating at the moment. Business matters that involve travel, anything to do with the export trade or any kind of foreign connection are likely to be a bit of a mess today. Murphy's Law will operate in connection with any kind of educational matter too, so expect to get nowhere with these kinds of project for now.

SATURDAY, 2ND JANUARY
Full Moon

Today's Full Moon shows that important decisions have to be made at a time of rapidly changing circumstances. News that arrives today could well be disturbing yet will prove to be a blessing in disguise in the long run. You may be considering a move of home, possibly to a distant location, or even throwing in your present career to take up an educational course of some kind. People you meet while travelling will have important words to say.

SUNDAY, 3RD JANUARY
Moon opposite Venus

Your life needs some kind of alteration or rearranging now. You may have too many burdens being placed upon you at the moment, both at home and at work, and you will need to sort these out soon before they break your back in two. You may need more help from those around you or you may have to take on some kind of staff to do some of your jobs for you.

MONDAY, 4TH JANUARY
Venus into Aquarius

This is a good day to begin new projects and to get great ideas off the ground. Venus is now moving into the area of your chart that is concerned with creativity, so over the next few weeks you can take advantage of this and get involved with some kind of creative process. Venus is concerned with the production of beauty, so utilize this planetary energy to enhance any of your creations.

TUESDAY, 5TH JANUARY
Venus conjunct Neptune

You can't see straight today and the world appears to be covered in a nice woolly haze. You may drift into love or into an affair without quite knowing how this happened. You may simply feel happy and content for no special reason. Your artistic and creative talents should come to the fore, because you are filled with great ideas for creative projects just now.

WEDNESDAY, 6TH JANUARY
Moon square Pluto

If you believe everything that you hear today, you will end up feeling worried or upset. Someone may have been making jealous or spiteful remarks behind your back and these will find their way back to you today. Alternatively, someone could try to persuade or manipulate you into doing something that they want but which is against your best interests.

THURSDAY, 7TH JANUARY
Mercury into Capricorn

The past exerts a powerful influence as Mercury enters the house of heritage.

LIBRA

You'll find that things long forgotten will somehow re-enter your life over the next couple of weeks. An interest in your family heritage may develop or possibly a new-found passion for antiques. Some good, meaningful conversations in the family will prove enlightening.

FRIDAY, 8TH JANUARY
Moon trine Venus

Your love life receives a welcome boost today as the Moon and Venus conspire to lift the passionate intensity. Being a creature of impulse it shouldn't be too much of a problem to arrange an evening of amorous dalliance. A trip to the theatre or cinema would bring a little sparkle into your relationship.

SATURDAY, 9TH JANUARY
Moon square Sun

Nostalgia and more than a touch of insecurity mingle as the Moon enters a stressful aspect with the sun today. You need some reassurance that your domestic and emotional life is safe and lasting. Any hint of change will be disturbing today so stick close to home and don't overload your schedule.

SUNDAY, 10TH JANUARY
Moon opposite Saturn

Other people seem to be landing you with a number of unwanted problems these days, because they want you to shoulder their responsibilities for them rather than making the effort to do this for themselves. You may have to deal with a really awkward person today, perhaps one of those 'It is more than my job's worth' kind of officials. Whatever the problem, you will have to put your foot down in order to prevent yourself from being pushed around or used.

MONDAY, 11TH JANUARY
Moon square Uranus

Children can be a trial, and those of you with offspring can expect to be landed with unexpected expense today. It may not have been their fault exactly, but you'll still have to carry the can for them. Hopefully, you won't have to dish out too much cash, but it must be pointed out that you are not going to make a habit of supplementing their spendthrift ways.

TUESDAY, 12TH JANUARY
Venus sextile Pluto

A letter or a phone call could change your life in a dramatic manner today. This may set you off on the start of a long and successful creative enterprise or it could be the start of a truly heaven-made romantic partnership. Business partnerships are well starred today, so whatever it is that you want to start doing, get going on it now!

WEDNESDAY, 13TH JANUARY
Venus conjunct Uranus

Almost anything could happen today and it probably will! New friends, new lovers and new interests seem to be crowding into your life now. If you can get away for a short holiday, then take that opportunity. This will be all the better if you can find somewhere really comfortable and luxurious to visit. You may fall headlong in love at around this time because you seem to be both terribly attractive and also very vulnerable.

THURSDAY, 14TH JANUARY
Sun sextile Jupiter

If you are asked to travel in connection with work, then do so. You may have to look at a few legal or official details in connection with career or home today. Your health should be improving.

FRIDAY, 15TH JANUARY
Sun square Mars

You may find family life a bit difficult at the moment. There may be too much for you to do within the home and not enough help and understanding from loved ones. Get out for a walk for a while today and leave them to get on with the washing-up for once.

SATURDAY, 16TH JANUARY
Moon conjunct Mercury

Your home is likely to be the meeting place for half your neighbourhood today. You may decide to throw a party or it may simply be that everybody seems to congregate in your kitchen today. News will flow as quickly as the drinks (or the tea and coffee) and the atmosphere will be light and cheerful.

SUNDAY, 17TH JANUARY
New Moon

The New Moon falls in the sphere of home and family today indicating a need for a change. For some reason you've been dissatisfied with your domestic set-up so you may consider looking at house prices in your own, or indeed another area. You probably feel that you need more space and light in your life which your present home isn't providing. A family member may be considering setting up home for themselves and deserves all the encouragement you can give.

MONDAY, 18TH JANUARY
Sun square Saturn

You may have already begun to realize that you cannot please all of the people all of the time, and it seems likely at the moment that you cannot please anyone at all! You may have to make some quite hard decisions about your partnerships and your family relationships, possibly even considering putting some distance between yourself and your partner or your relatives.

TUESDAY, 19TH JANUARY
Moon conjunct Venus

This should be a fun-packed day. The Moon and Venus get together in the most pleasurable area of your chart surrounding you with friendly faces and a lot of laughs. Female companionship is particularly stimulating and will increase your self-confidence and belief in your talents. For the romantically inclined, attractions of a physical nature abound.

WEDNESDAY, 20TH JANUARY
Sun into Aquarius

You are going to be in a slightly frivolous frame of mind over the next few weeks and you shouldn't punish yourself for this. Pay attention to a creative interest or a demanding hobby or involving yourself in something creative on behalf of others. A couple of typical examples would be the production of a school play or making preparations for a flower and vegetable show.

THURSDAY, 21ST JANUARY
Mars opposite Saturn

The path of true love rarely runs completely smoothly and today is one of those days where there are stones and obstacles placed on your road. Your lover may be too busy working to spend much time with you; alternatively, both of you have family responsibilities that are getting in the way of your relationship. This will soon pass.

FRIDAY, 22ND JANUARY
Sun conjunct Neptune

Romance may strike quite suddenly, and from a most unexpected quarter! You may find yourself literally tripping up over someone really wonderful. The problem is that you are not looking at anything really clearly at the moment and you may mistake someone's intentions. The chances are that you are the one who is being cool and calm while someone else suddenly decides that you are the nicest and cutest thing around.

SATURDAY, 23RD JANUARY
Mercury sextile Jupiter

If you need help either at home or at work, this will be forthcoming today. In fact, this is a good day in which to hire someone for a specific task either on the short or the long term. This is also an excellent time in which to buy yourself some kind of labour-saving gadget or appliance or some kind of office equipment.

SUNDAY, 24TH JANUARY
Mercury square Saturn

A parent or an older person may need quite a bit of your attention today and you may not have it to spare. Your mood is a somewhat ratty and tense and it wouldn't take much for you to become extremely upset. You need to rest a bit more, even if it doesn't altogether suit those who are around you, you must do something to relax your nerves soon.

MONDAY, 25TH JANUARY
Moon square Uranus

Be prepared for sudden setbacks or moments of family tension today. There may be disagreements about who has the right to spend the family money and on what kind of items. Children or young people may spring surprises on you and these may be of a kind that you would rather do without. A friend may dump his or her children on you just when you had planned a nice rest for yourself.

TUESDAY, 26TH JANUARY
Mars into Scorpio

Mars moves into your Solar house of finance and income from today and draws your attention to urgent matters that should have been dealt with long ago. If you've let your economic realities slide, then now is the time to rectify the situation before the expense becomes unbearable. You can focus an abundance of energy towards increasing your income now, review expenditures and make much needed economies. Swift action is your forte.

WEDNESDAY, 27TH JANUARY
Venus sextile Saturn

Initially, romantic prospects are cooled by the influence of Saturn; however, loving Venus comes to the rescue and solves all problems. The latter half of the day is excellent for affairs of the heart.

LIBRA

THURSDAY, 28TH JANUARY
Venus into Pisces

Venus moves out of the fun, sun and pleasure area of your chart into the work, duty and health area, and it will stay there for the next few weeks. This suggests that any problems related to work and duty will become easier to handle and also that you could start to see some kind of practical outcome from all that you have been doing lately. If you have been off-colour recently, Venus will help you to feel better soon.

FRIDAY, 29TH JANUARY
Venus trine Mars

You have tremendous energy today and will be quite prepared to delve deeply into any problem that confronts you. You won't be content to accept the easy answer to anything and will probe to the heart of any matter. This is a day for problem solving!

SATURDAY, 30TH JANUARY
Sun sextile Pluto

You may read something or be told something that makes a strong impression on you today. There may be good news in connection with children and young people too.

SUNDAY, 31ST JANUARY
Full Moon eclipse

Eclipses have had an evil reputation throughout history and the Romans were particularly wary of them, but an eclipse is only really likely to cause trouble if it falls in a sensitive spot on your own birthchart. In any case, there are usually about four of them in any year, so they cannot be all that important. However, today's eclipse may bring a problem to a head in connection with a romance or in connection with a younger member of the family.

February at a Glance

LOVE	❤	❤	❤	❤	
WORK	★	★	★	★	
MONEY	£	£	£	£	£
HEALTH	✪	✪	✪	✪	
LUCK	♘	♘	♘	♘	

LIBRA

MONDAY, 1ST FEBRUARY
Mars square Neptune

It would be a serious mistake to act on impulse today. Every move you make should be carefully thought out because your own enthusiasms could lead you astray and prompt you into some very unwise investments. Take care!

TUESDAY, 2ND FEBRUARY
Sun conjunct Uranus

The Sun's conjunction with Uranus shows that you're in a break-out mood! You'll be so innovative and eccentric that you'll be bound to attract attention wherever you go! Most of this will be extremely flattering since your essential personality will shine through as you sever the bond that could have held you back!

WEDNESDAY, 3RD FEBRUARY
Sun conjunct Mercury

Communication is the name of the game today as this will enhance all your relationships. You could have a really enjoyable chat to a friend or you could sit and talk things over with your lover today. You may decide to start a creative venture now, if so, this is the time to do some research on your ideas and to see what materials and methods would best suit your purpose.

THURSDAY, 4TH FEBRUARY
Moon opposite Jupiter

You're rather tired today. It's possible that you've been taking on too much just to show how impressive you can be. Are you sure that you're not playing the martyr and going for the sympathy vote? It doesn't really matter because the fact remains that you could do with a quiet undemanding day, so make sure you get one.

FRIDAY, 5TH FEBRUARY
Mercury conjunct Uranus

There could be some really spectacular news today, possibly in connection with children and young people. You may hear something unexpected about brothers, sisters or other members of the family. If you are involved in any kind of creative project, today could mark the kind of breakthrough that you have been waiting for. The same thing applies to any kind of mechanical or engineering problem, in that you should be able to find the answers to practical problems now.

SATURDAY, 6TH FEBRUARY
Venus square Pluto

This could be quite a difficult day at work in which you suffer from someone else's attempts to manipulate you or to manoeuvre a situation around to suit them. Be on guard against sexual harassment today. Use your own power sparingly too, because too much weight-throwing will alienate others.

SUNDAY, 7TH FEBRUARY
Moon conjunct Mars

You've got the energy and drive to make the most out of your cash flow today. The Lunar conjunction with Mars in the most financially aware area of your chart helps you to overcome any monetary crisis. A sudden boost to your income could come through a job or investment opportunity. As with all Mars aspects, this one warns against acting on impulse.

MONDAY, 8TH FEBRUARY
Moon square Sun

Go easy on your expenditure today. Avoid the shops, don't go looking for bargains and don't let anybody else talk you into buying anything either. Older relatives may be a bit irritating, possibly because they need you to do something for them which eats into your spare time. It would be better to spend today attending to your duties rather than to seek out amusements.

TUESDAY, 9TH FEBRUARY
Moon trine Jupiter

You have the leisure to take some time to look at the financial realities of your life today. Though the picture may not be as bright as you'd wish, you'll soon see that improvements can be made. I'm not just talking about budgeting here; you may have been thinking about a new post which would be more lucrative. If so, you'll make up your mind to take it now.

WEDNESDAY, 10TH FEBRUARY
Moon sextile Uranus

There will be some really unexpected news today, and this may come from the direction of relatives or neighbours. Fortunately, the news is good, and this will assure you that your friends and relatives are healthy and happy. You may suddenly find yourself becoming attracted to an interesting and intelligent stranger.

THURSDAY, 11TH FEBRUARY
Mercury sextile Saturn

You'll really fancy the idea of having good time but those around you are equally keen to remind you of your duties and responsibilities. You may have to do things for others rather than for yourself for a while.

FRIDAY, 12TH FEBRUARY
Mercury into Pisces

The movement of Mercury into your Solar sixth house of work, duties and health suggests that a slightly more serious phase is on the way. Over the next three weeks or so you will have to concentrate on what needs to be done rather than on having a good time. You may have a fair bit to do with neighbours, colleagues and relatives of your own age group, spending more than the usual amount of time on the phone to them.

SATURDAY, 13TH FEBRUARY
Jupiter into Aries

You'll experience a deep need for companionship in the coming months as Jupiter moves into your Solar area of partnerships from today. Solitude is the last thing you want now and you will go to great lengths to make sure that you are never lonely.

SUNDAY, 14TH FEBRUARY
Moon sextile Jupiter

St Valentine's Day is a great time to spend with your lover. A feeling of togetherness is obvious, add to this some soft lights and music and you have the perfect recipe for romance. A perfect gesture of affection will set your hearts aglow.

MONDAY, 15TH FEBRUARY
Moon conjunct Uranus

(If you are male, over the age of a hundred or under the age of two, don't bother to read this!) The planets are playing havoc with your hormones today. You could find yourself suddenly and inexplicably pregnant despite the pills you swallow and the devices you use to ensure that this doesn't happen. You may already be happily pregnant, only to be told that it is twins! If pregnancy is not possible then you could fall suddenly and devastatingly in love. In short, this is a great day for any kind of fate worse than death!

TUESDAY, 16TH FEBRUARY
New Moon eclipse

Eclipses are quite difficult things to live with. The Romans used to dread them, saying that they brought bad times in their wake. However, there are usually two Lunar and two Solar eclipses each year so they aren't that unusual. Problems come when these fall on sensitive areas of one's birthchart. If this eclipse catches you out, then it will cut short a celebration or some kind of leisure activity.

LIBRA

WEDNESDAY, 17TH FEBRUARY
Sun sextile Saturn

You may feel that you would like to be treated like a king or a queen today and, fortunately, your nearest and dearest will be happy to fulfil your regal dreams and demands. Lucky old you!

THURSDAY, 18TH FEBRUARY
Mercury square Pluto

Brothers and sisters may be in a bit of a mess just now and you may be called upon to help them out. A relative of around your own age may ask for some financial help and you may be tempted to lend them money. Take a tip from us – don't lend them anything but give them a lesser amount as an outright gift. This way, there will be no bad feelings on either side from a loan not being repaid.

FRIDAY, 19TH FEBRUARY
Sun into Pisces

The Sun moves into your Solar sixth house of work and duty for the next month. This Solar movement will also encourage you to concentrate on your health and well-being and also that of your family. If you are off-colour, the Sun will help you to get back to full health once again. If you have jobs that need to be done, the next month or so will be a good time to get them done.

SATURDAY, 20TH FEBRUARY
Void Moon

This is one of those days when none of the planets is making any worthwhile kind of aspect to any of the others. Even the Moon is 'void of course', which means that it is not making any aspects of importance to the other planets. On such a day, avoid starting anything new important. Do what needs to be done and take some time off for a rest.

SUNDAY, 21ST FEBRUARY
Venus into Aries

Venus, the planet of romance, moves into your horoscope area of close relationships from today increasing your physical desires and bringing the light of love into your heart. If you're involved in a long-term partnership, it is a chance to renew the magic of the early days of your union. If single, then the next few weeks should bring a stunning new attraction into your life.

LIBRA

MONDAY, 22ND FEBRUARY
Venus sextile Neptune

You could find allies in the most unlikely of places today. Other people will be kind and thoughtful in their dealings with you. Women, in particular, will be on hand to help you sort out a muddling and confusing situation. Your artistic and creative side is coming to the fore now and you could see just how to make something beautiful for your home or as a gift for someone else.

TUESDAY, 23RD FEBRUARY
Moon opposite Pluto

While there seems to be a good deal of news from afar, actual travel plans could become temporarily fouled up. Try to avoid getting involved with legal matters of any kind today, because these would not go too well just now. It seems that there is someone behind the scenes who is trying to manipulate a situation in a way that may not be entirely in your interests.

WEDNESDAY, 24TH FEBRUARY
Venus conjunct Jupiter

A conjunction between lovely Venus and the amazingly expansive Jupiter suggests that something important is happening in your Solar seventh house of partnerships. Your favourite member of the opposite sex could choose today to pop the question! If this is not appropriate, then try to spend some time alone with your partner because you will enjoy each other's company to the full.

THURSDAY, 25TH FEBRUARY
Moon trine Sun

In all career affairs, today should be smooth sailing. Harmony reigns with your bosses and co-workers so no matter how arduous the task you'll find that everyone is in agreement. Many hands make light work and for once you are perfectly content to carry on with routine duties. It may not be an exciting outlook but it is familiar and you'll be quite comfortable with that.

FRIDAY, 26TH FEBRUARY
Sun trine Mars

Since you feel so good, you can turn your mind to work habits and financial affairs. At last you have the energy to tackle problems that have been lurking in the background for some time. You're bound to be successful in any endeavour today.

SATURDAY, 27TH FEBRUARY
Jupiter sextile Neptune

There's a highly romantic, not to say passionate, influence from today's aspect between Jupiter and Neptune. These planets may indicate an affair of a lifetime! Or at least it seems like it! Neptune, doesn't generally promote realism, but at least the fantasy will be extremely enjoyable while it lasts!

SUNDAY, 28TH FEBRUARY
Moon opposite Uranus

Friends may let you down today and, while they may not do this deliberately, the results of their actions could be extremely irritating. Children or younger members of the family may be upset or unhappy about something, and you may have to make a special effort to get them to talk about what is bothering them.

March at a Glance

LOVE	❤	❤	❤	❤	❤
WORK	★				
MONEY	£	£	£	£	
HEALTH	✚	✚			
LUCK	☋	☋	☋		

MONDAY, 1ST MARCH
Saturn into Taurus

You have got a curious view of money at the moment. When you have it you seem to get rid of the stuff as quickly as possible and when the coffers are empty, you blame yourself for being extravagant.

TUESDAY, 2ND MARCH
Mercury into Aries

The inquisitive Mercury moves into your Solar house of marriage and long-lasting relationships from today. It ushers in a period when a renewed understanding can be reached between yourself and your partner. New relationships can be formed under this influence too, though these will tend to be on a light, fairly superficial level. Good humour and plenty of charm should be a feature for a few weeks, though you must try to curb a tendency to needlessly criticize another's foibles. Remember, not even you are perfect!

WEDNESDAY, 3RD MARCH
Venus trine Pluto

This is a great time to open the lines of communication between you and your lover. If you feel that things haven't quite been going the way you would like them to go, then sit down quietly and explain how you feel and also really listen to what your partner has to say. This way, you could begin to reach some kind of real agreement and avoid future misunderstandings.

THURSDAY, 4TH MARCH
Venus sextile Uranus

You may kick the traces over today and do something that is completely out of character. You could suddenly take off with a friend to enjoy an unusual day out or even disappear off the map for a while. Take a last-minute holiday with a pal maybe.

FRIDAY, 5TH MARCH
Mercury sextile Neptune

Friends will come to your aid today. You may feel like helping others but they will also be in the mood to give you a hand. You may not actually need any kind of practical help, and your friends will realize this by giving you just the kind of emotional uplift and encouragement that you need just now. Your confidence level is beginning to creep upwards at long last.

SATURDAY, 6TH MARCH
Moon square Neptune

Don't let dreams get in the way of reality today because your imagination may intrude onto those occasions when you should have your wits about you. Be sure to take any words of love that are poured into your shell-like ear with a large pinch of salt!

SUNDAY, 7TH MARCH
Moon square Uranus

You may have to put a pet project onto the back burner for a while. Perhaps a friend cannot give you the help and support that you expected, either through lack of time or sudden loss of interest. You may suddenly lose interest in a particular plan yourself now.

LIBRA

MONDAY, 8TH MARCH
Moon trine Venus

Social opportunities are all around you now, so don't sit around on your own when there are people out there who'd welcome your company. Pop into a neglected friend's for a cup of tea and a chat; you'll be glad you made the effort as well as cheering up someone who needs it. Pick up the phone and ring a distant friend or one or two of your relatives for a good old gossip today.

TUESDAY, 9TH MARCH
Moon trine Jupiter

Your home and domestic circumstances are really rather good today and whatever you have in mind will go particularly well. You may be keen to move house or to put your own home into some kind of new order and now is the time to get this into action. Your partner will have good news in connection with money or business matters and this too will help to ease any financial burdens in the home.

WEDNESDAY, 10TH MARCH
Mercury retrograde

In all partnerships, both business and personal misunderstandings, cross-purposes and ill-timed words are likely today because Mercury embarks on a retrograde course. The next few weeks should see a lot of confusion. You must be as clear as crystal in all you say, otherwise arguments will result simply because one or other will have caught the wrong end of the stick.

THURSDAY, 11TH MARCH
Moon square Mercury

No sooner does Mercury open channels of communication than you're back into a cycle of misunderstanding and mistrust. Perhaps you need greater clarity of speech. Take it slowly, wounds don't heal in ten minutes, so it is still important to gently renew the trust.

FRIDAY, 12TH MARCH
Moon sextile Mars

It is time to take a serious look at your cash situation. Any attention paid to savings schemes, investments, insurance policies, tax affairs and the like will stand you in good stead for the future. You have to look to the interests of your whole family now and take the long-term view; you won't lose out by it.

LIBRA

SATURDAY, 13TH MARCH
Mercury sextile Neptune

Treat yourself and your lover to a night out. An evening at the movies followed by a romantic candle-lit supper would be a dream come true. Failing that, a cuddle on the sofa would be equally acceptable.

SUNDAY, 14TH MARCH
Moon sextile Pluto

Your emotional condition does not depend upon the moods or the behaviour of others now and you seem to be in charge of your own destiny at the moment. The needs and requirements of those who are around you are important and these have to be taken into consideration, but not at the expense of your own needs and requirements at the moment. You seem to be moving full steam ahead with something good.

MONDAY, 15TH MARCH
Moon sextile Venus

It is a day of relaxation, but not necessarily of calm. The Lunar aspect of Venus puts you in a sensual mood, determined to enjoy the finer things of life. Good food, good wines and the company of someone you love are the recipe for perfect bliss. It doesn't matter what you do, as long as you enjoy it. Give yourself over to absolute pleasure today.

TUESDAY, 16TH MARCH
Moon square Pluto

Something could come to light today that has been quietly going wrong for a little while now. This is not a big deal, nor is it anything to worry about, but something, either in connection with your health or with a mechanical item needs to be fixed soon. If you know that your vehicle is playing up, then get this mended before the problem grows into a really expensive one.

WEDNESDAY, 17TH MARCH
New Moon

Today's New Moon gives you the stamina to shrug off any minor ailments that have been troubling you. Occurring, as it does, in your Solar house of health and work, it is obvious that you need to get yourself into shape to face the challenges that await you. A few early nights, a better diet and a readiness to give up bad habits such as smoking will work wonders.

LIBRA

THURSDAY, 18TH MARCH
Venus into Taurus

Venus enters the area of your chart that is closely involved with love and sex today. Oddly enough, this aspect can bring the end of a difficult relationship or it can just as easily herald the start of a wonderful new one. If you have been dating but haven't yet got around to 'mating', this could be the start of something wonderful. Your emotional life over the next two or three weeks should be something to remember, that's for sure!

FRIDAY, 19TH MARCH
Sun conjunct Mercury

You will be a source of wonder today as you effortlessly tackle anything and everything that the world can throw at you. The Sun's conjunction with Mercury puts a powerful emphasis on your house of work so this is the time to improve your prospects and generally make your way up the ladder of success. This is a good day to attend interviews and to give your views and ideas a fair hearing. You can't afford to sit back and wait any longer, so don't hide your light under a bushel.

SATURDAY, 20TH MARCH
Venus conjunct Saturn

Monetary concerns are likely to give you a few anxious moments today because you'll be painfully aware of your shortcomings in economic planning. If you're sensible, you can take this minor shock as a positive impulse to get things sorted out. You have the chance to put yourself on a firm cash footing, but you do have to be methodical and not allow anything to be left to chance. Some expert advice should be sought now, before the situation gets out of hand.

SUNDAY, 21ST MARCH
Sun into Aries

The Sun moves into the area of your chart devoted to relationships from today. If things have been difficult in a personal or in business partnerhship, then this is your chance to put things right. It is obvious that the significant other in your life deserves respect and affection and that's just what you're now prepared to give. Teamwork is the key to success over the next month.

MONDAY, 22ND MARCH
Moon trine Neptune

You are in a daft and dreamy state of mind today and it will be hard for you to get your head together or to deal with anything sensible. You seem keen to escape from the drudgery of everyday life and you want to dream of romance, far-distant shores and of winning a large sum on the lottery. We hope your dreams come true!

TUESDAY, 23RD MARCH
Venus square Neptune

We all know that there is a time and a place for everything but there isn't any time or any place that is right for anything today. You are in a muddle and nothing you can do seems likely to straighten things out. Romantic affairs are likely to go sadly wrong now and sexual matters could be a real minefield. Perhaps it would be better to avoid love, sex and romance for the time being.

WEDNESDAY, 24TH MARCH
Moon square Sun

This is one of those days when you wish you had stayed in bed! There are potential difficulties all around you now and it will take all your attempts at tact and charm to get others to behave decently. All those who should, by rights, be on your side will lack any urge to co-operate and your usual sources of sympathy will dry up.

THURSDAY, 25TH MARCH
Sun sextile Neptune

You seem set to become the star attraction in your circle somehow today, and you may find yourself doing something that makes you shine in front of others. You may be the most popular boy or girl at the local disco or the most exciting rider on the go-cart track. There is a slightly crazy feel to this day and you will come out of it feeling exhilarated and excited by the events that it brings.

FRIDAY, 26TH MARCH
Moon square Saturn

A private problem could be more worrying than you're prepared to admit today. Though you'll want to put a brave face on things for your friends, the truth is that you can't get your anxiety out of your mind. I think you'd be doing yourself a favour if you confided your trouble to someone you trust. After all, two heads are better than one.

SATURDAY, 27TH MARCH
Venus opposite Mars

Money is the root of all evil and it will cause an argument or two today. Agreements are hard to come by, and even those that do are likely to be worthless. Don't enter into any hire-purchase agreements or sign contracts just now.

LIBRA

SUNDAY, 28TH MARCH
Void Moon

Occasionally one finds a day during which neither the planets nor the Moon make any major aspects to each other and on such a day the Moon's course is said to be 'void'. There is nothing wrong with a day like this but there is no point in trying to start anything new or important because there isn't enough of a planetary boost to get it off the ground. Stick to your normal routine.

MONDAY, 29TH MARCH
Moon square Pluto

You know in your heart that something isn't right and until you find out exactly what is going on, it will be hard to know what action you should take. Wait until you hear a bit more before making up your mind.

TUESDAY, 30TH MARCH
Jupiter trine Pluto

Hold on to your hat because today's stars definitely add a passionate angle to your life. If you have any energy left after such sensual gymnastics, Jupiter and Pluto promote a sharing of your deepest feelings.

WEDNESDAY, 31ST MARCH
Full Moon

The Full Moon in your sign shows that you've come to the end of a personal phase and that it is time to tie up the loose ends and move on. This should be an opportunity to rid yourself of harmful little habits and create a whole new persona. This could be an image transformation. So, if you're at all dissatisfied by the way you present yourself to the world, then work out your own personal make-over. You'll be astounded by the reception the new you gets.

April at a Glance

LOVE	❤	❤	❤	
WORK	★	★	★	
MONEY	£	£	£	£
HEALTH	✚			
LUCK	♘	♘		

THURSDAY, 1ST APRIL
Sun conjunct Jupiter

Everything to do with partnerships or relationships is going well just now. You may meet someone who will have a profound influence on your life. This may be the start of a really productive working alliance or a fun-filled and very loving new relationship. If you are happily settled, there will be great news of a lucky and advantageous kind for you and your lover.

FRIDAY, 2ND APRIL
Mercury direct

You should feel less on edge and generally more healthy as Mercury gets back into his proper course from today. A friend may be applying pressure to get you to do something that you're not at all keen on. Fortunately Mercury's forward motion should ensure that you have the eloquence to defuse the situation without ruffling any feathers.

SATURDAY, 3RD APRIL
Moon conjunct Mars

There should be great news about financial matters today. If you have been waiting for something to come in, it should arrive now. If you are looking for an opportunity to earn more, this should be on the way now too. A young man may help you to mend something that you rely on and he may also be able to point you in the direction of a real bargain.

SUNDAY, 4TH APRIL
Mercury sextile Venus

You will have to put yourself out on behalf of others today but they will appreciate what you are doing for them and they will return the favour when they can. A phone call, letter or comment about your performance at work will cheer you up.

MONDAY, 5TH APRIL
Moon sextile Neptune

You won't want to be distracted today since you'll discover a subject that you'll know instinctively to be for you. You won't rest until you've found out more, and enjoy every second of your discoveries.

TUESDAY, 6TH APRIL
Saturn square Neptune

Boring duty calls when you least want to deal with the trials and tribulations of everyday life! You'd rather be far away indulging your dreams and floating in a sea of romance. Unfortunately, some things are just too pressing to be ignored! Blame it on Saturn the hard taskmaster of the zodiac!

WEDNESDAY, 7TH APRIL
Sun sextile Uranus

This is a good time to make new friends and to join with others in partnership projects of all kinds, especially those that aren't attached directly to your work or your personal life. Therefore, any clubs, societies or group activities that attract you now could be extremely useful to you in a number of ways in the future.

THURSDAY, 8TH APRIL
Moon sextile Mars

Your sense of security is boosted today as you've rarely felt so safe and content. The influence of your family is a strong factor in this as they soothe away all fears. If you can be bothered to emerge from this aura of tranquillity long enough to count costs and do your books, you'll find that your financial position is in a better state than you'd imagined.

FRIDAY, 9TH APRIL
Moon sextile Mercury

Good news! If you are waiting for something to be fixed at home or at work, it will be. Frustrations will melt away as friends, neighbours and relatives rush round to help out with all those minor chores and problems that are plaguing you. A neighbourhood event may provide some unexpected amusement and pals who pop in may provide some more.

SATURDAY, 10TH APRIL
Moon square Saturn

You may be a little worried about the health of a younger family member today. Keep any sick youngsters firmly in doors, let them watch what they want on the television and give them something nice to eat. Your children or grandchildren are not malingering, they may be tired or worried and they need a little extra sympathy and love today.

SUNDAY, 11TH APRIL
Moon sextile Sun

Love is on your agenda today so, whether you are in the throes of a fresh and new love affair or in a happily settled in a relationship of long standing, all dealings with your other half will make you happy now. This is not the time for doubts.

LIBRA

MONDAY, 12TH APRIL
Venus into Gemini

Venus enters your Solar ninth house of exploration this month making you slightly restless. Venus is concerned with the pleasures of life and leisure activities of all kinds, so explore such ideas as your sporting interests, listening to interesting music or going to art galleries and the like. You may want to travel somewhere new and interesting soon.

TUESDAY, 13TH APRIL
Moon sextile Venus

You seem to be in some kind of dilemma now, possibly due to a conflict between what you need, what is needed from you by your bosses or by those who think you owe them something, and also by your lover or partner in life. You cannot please everybody so you should work out a sensible compromise arrangement and make everyone aware that you intend to stick to this.

WEDNESDAY, 14TH APRIL
Moon into Aries

The accent is on close relationships today. It is a good opportunity to show by a small but telling gesture how much your other half means to you. Show your appreciation and give in to a romantic impulse and let there be no uncertainty about the depth of your love. If you're single, this is one of those times when love could enter your life.

THURSDAY, 15TH APRIL
Moon conjunct Jupiter

You seem to be going through a rather good spell and this rather lucky phase will spill over into the lives of those whom you are closely associated with. Your partner could have as much luck and good news as you do just now. This is a great time to get together with others and even to make plans for a future life together with the one you love.

FRIDAY, 16TH APRIL
New Moon

The only planetary activity today is a New Moon in your opposite sign. It is possible that this could bring the start of a new relationship for the lonely but, to be honest, this planetary aspect is a bit too weak for such a big event. It is much more likely that you will improve on a current relationship rather than start a new one at this time.

LIBRA

SATURDAY, 17TH APRIL
Mercury into Aries

Mercury moves into the area of your chart which is concerned with relationships that are open and above-board now. This suggests that over the next few weeks you will have nothing to be secretive about in connection with your relationships with others. Your friendships will be free and easy and your lovers the kind whom you can happily take home to mother!

SUNDAY, 18TH APRIL
Moon conjunct Venus

Today's stars promise nothing but harmony and contentment. The Moon makes a splendid contact with Venus on Friday 23rd April and bestows the ability to enjoy life to its fullest. Any past family difficulties, such as rows with in-laws, can now be put behind you and oil poured on troubled waters. You'll feel at one with the world.

MONDAY, 19TH APRIL
Mars opposite Saturn

Financial problems loom large today and you could lose all sense of proportion and panic unnecessarily if you don't keep your feet on the ground. OK, so the picture looks grim at the moment, but the solution to this worry is sensible budgeting not flapping around like a flag in the wind.

TUESDAY, 20TH APRIL
Sun into Taurus

Today, the Sun enters your Solar eighth house of beginnings and endings. Thus, over the next month, you can expect something to wind its way to a conclusion, while something else starts to take its place. This doesn't seem to signify a major turning point or any really big event in your life but it does mark one of those small turning points that we all go through from time to time.

WEDNESDAY, 21ST APRIL
Venus opposite Pluto

Money will slip through your fingers today so keep away from the shops, don't look at any catalogues and ignore all advertisements on the television. This way, you may avoid unnecessary spending, but we wouldn't bet on it!

THURSDAY, 22ND APRIL
Mercury sextile Neptune

Enjoyment is the name of the game today. If you are involved in a long-term partnership, then treat yourself and your lover to an evening on the town. If you are solo, then get socializing and you may not be in that state much longer!

FRIDAY, 23RD APRIL
Jupiter sextile Uranus

You are likely to be swept off your feet today! A major love interest is set to come into your life very soon and knock your emotions sideways in the process! Jupiter and Uranus inspire sudden romance now and it may be a journey or contact with foreigners that sets this off.

SATURDAY, 24TH APRIL
Sun opposite Mars

A large bill could send you into an uncontrollable fury today, which you'll agree is not good for your blood pressure. Take some deep breaths and try to calm down for goodness sake! If you need to discuss money with a partner, either do this very calmly indeed or, if that isn't possible, leave your chat until you are in an easier frame of mind.

SUNDAY, 25TH APRIL
Moon trine Saturn

The aspect between the Moon and Saturn shows that you're in desperate need of some relaxation. Stress levels run high at the moment, but though you've got the stamina to cope with them, you should be kind to yourself too. Money worries are common under this aspect as are troublesome emotional undercurrents. Give yourself some peace and quiet, away from disturbing influences and the solutions will occur to you that much sooner.

MONDAY, 26TH APRIL
Mercury trine Pluto

You are in an oddly artful mood today and, if you cannot get your own way by direct means, you will be able to find some kind of indirect way of getting what you want out of others. You could be very kittenish just now but even the sweetest of kittens have sharp claws.

TUESDAY, 27TH APRIL
Sun conjunct Saturn

You are taking a serious look at those who are close to you and deciding whether you wish to continue dealing with them in the same old way or whether you need to change your tactics now.

WEDNESDAY, 28TH APRIL
Moon opposite Mercury

Be careful of what you say now, since your tongue wags so readily that you could let an important secret slip. A private revelation between you and your spouse will do more good than otherwise, but don't air personal affairs in public.

THURSDAY, 29TH APRIL
Mercury sextile Uranus

You may be swept off your feet by someone whose charm, intelligence and humour takes your heart by storm. This may only be a passing fancy but it is very enjoyable nevertheless.

FRIDAY, 30TH APRIL
Full Moon

Today's full Moon seems to be highlighting a minor problem in connection with financial matters today. You may have been overspending recently and this could be the cause of your current financial embarrassment but there does seem to be something deeper to be considered here. Perhaps the firm you work for has a temporary problem or maybe your partner is a bit short of cash just now.

May at a Glance

LOVE	❤				
WORK	★	★	★	★	★
MONEY	£	£	£		
HEALTH	✪	✪			
LUCK	☊	☊			

SATURDAY, 1ST MAY
Mercury conjunct Jupiter

This should be a lucky and a happy day for both you and your partner and, oh boy, you could do with it! There will be good news about money matters for either or both of you and if either one of you has been out of work, there will be news of a good job opportunity. You may start to plan a holiday and/or make other optimistic plans for the future.

SUNDAY, 2ND MAY
Moon sextile Neptune

Your delicacy of expression and tactful words could win the heart of a new love today. Even if you have no intention of any amorous involvement it'll be pleasant to know that you can still turn a head or two.

MONDAY, 3RD MAY
Moon sextile Uranus

One or two of your friends are about to spring a pleasant surprise on you and there could be interesting and exciting news now, possibly also involving friends. You may hear good news about a project that you have been working towards, giving you the feeling that you are travelling down the right road at last.

TUESDAY, 4TH MAY
Moon opposite Venus

You seem to be giving up the thought of becoming a hard-headed business person today and becoming a dreamy, sensitive and kindly soul instead. Your soft centre is showing through your usual crusty exterior and your response to others will be tender and affectionate. This is a marvellous day in which to whisper sweet nothings to your lover and also to steer clear of any serious negotiating.

WEDNESDAY, 5TH MAY
Mars into Libra

Mars enters your own sign of the zodiac today and it will spend a few weeks there, bringing zest, energy and a welcome element of fun into your life. You seem to be on a 'roll' at the moment and, as long as you keep up the momentum, there is no reason why you should not be able to reach your objectives.

THURSDAY, 6TH MAY
Moon square Jupiter

You could be torn between different members of your family today because they all seem to need your attention at the same time. Added to this, is the fact that people outside of the home are also in need of your time and your attention and it is hard to cope with all these conflicting demands at once. Part of the problem may be that each of these people need money from you and all at the same time.

FRIDAY, 7TH MAY
Neptune retrograde

Neptune turns to retrograde motion in the Solar house of your horoscope that is concerned with creativity and amusements. If you fancy the kind of love affair that is amusing, exciting and totally lacking in responsibility, the best advice that we can give to you is to leave it for another time! If you are free to have such an affair, you could find yourself more deeply involved with the other person than you had bargained for. If you are not really free to indulge your passions, then hold off from doing so for the time being.

SATURDAY, 8TH MAY
Mercury into Taurus

Mercury moves into one of the most sensitive areas of your chart from today. Anything of an intimate nature from your physical relationships to the state of your bank balance comes under scrutiny now. Turn your heightened perceptions to your love life, important partnerships, and any affair that deals with investment, insurance, tax or shared resources. An intelligent approach now will save you a lot of problems later.

SUNDAY, 9TH MAY
Mercury sextile Venus

There's a highly romantic outlook today. The Lunar aspect to Venus puts you in a sentimental and loving frame of mind. You'll be anxious to share all spare time with a lover. If you're inclined to amorous conquest, you are guaranteed the response you desire. Your love life aside, those who are involved in delicate negotiations of any kind will find that diplomacy and charm will win the day.

MONDAY, 10TH MAY
Moon square Pluto

You may go about things with a touch of ruthlessness today. This mood can be beneficial if, for instance, you decide to clear out your wardrobe or clear up your working area. In such a mood, you will toss out all that junk that you have been keeping 'just in case' or all those pieces of paper that clutter the place up. On the other hand, you could deal ruthlessly with others.

TUESDAY, 11TH MAY
Mercury square Neptune

Not a good day to share intimate confidences or to talk over financial affairs with a relative stranger. If you do, you'll soon find that your most private business has become general knowledge! Keep your lip zipped!

WEDNESDAY, 12TH MAY
Moon trine Pluto

Your relationships with others are beginning to move into a much better phase now. It may be you, yourself, that is coming around to other people's way of thinking, or it may be others who are coming around to meet you half-way. You could discover that someone who you had considered as nothing more than a friend, colleague or a neighbour is beginning to mean much more to you.

THURSDAY, 13TH MAY
Mercury conjunct Saturn

There is a chance that you will be dealing with people who wear uniforms today. This may take you into contact with the police, firefighters or paramedics but it could also bring you close to someone who plays in a band or who wears a chef's outfit for work. This could also be a day of beginnings and endings, in which you find yourself mentally changing direction in some quite dramatic manner.

FRIDAY, 14TH MAY
Moon sextile Venus

The link between the Moon and Venus adds a compelling and seductive quality to your nature now. Since you're quick on the uptake, it won't take you long to realize that you're in a position to twist anyone around your little finger. A small flirtation today will gain you far more than any number of confrontations.

SATURDAY, 15TH MAY
New Moon

Apart from a new Moon today, there are no major planetary happenings. This suggests that you avoid making major changes in your life just now but make a couple of fresh starts in very minor matters. You may feel like taking your partner to task over their irritating ways, but perhaps today is not the best day for this.

SUNDAY, 16TH MAY
Venus sextile Saturn

Money and business take centre stage today, and don't you forget it! Though your mind is on some pleasurable possibilities, the real action lies with firm economic planning and career ambitions. This is no time for frivolity because many serious concerns require your immediate attention. Negotiations for loans, mortgages or legal affairs have to take priority now. The going may be slow, but vitally necessary.

MONDAY, 17TH MAY
Mercury square Uranus

This could be quite a disagreeable day as far as personal relationships are concerned. Some hurtful or tactless words could be spoken. However, you shouldn't make an issue of this since reaction would only make things worse.

LIBRA

TUESDAY, 18TH MAY
Moon sextile Saturn

Parents, parental figures or older people generally could help you climb over a particular hurdle. If these folks have been in business in the past or are running a business of their own at the moment, they will be in a good position to give you useful advice.

WEDNESDAY, 19TH MAY
Moon square Jupiter

The demands of the career go against your desire for some harmony at home today. Your relationship holds the key to your happiness but you may find it rather difficult to spend much time with your loved one just now.

THURSDAY, 20TH MAY
Moon opposite Neptune

It seems to be very hard for you to reach your objectives. Perhaps you feel off-colour, maybe you are just tired or simply not in the mood to make much effort. You have some really great ideas but the time does not seem to be right for you to put them into action. Maybe you don't really want to?

FRIDAY, 21ST MAY
Sun into Gemini

The Sun moves into your Solar ninth house today and it will stay there for a month. This would be a good time to travel overseas or to explore new neighbourhoods. It is also a good time to take up an interest in spiritual matters. You may find yourself keen to read about religious or philosophical subjects or even to explore the world of psychic healing over the next month or so.

SATURDAY, 22ND MAY
Uranus retrograde

The large and slow-moving planet, Uranus, turns to retrograde motion today and it will stay there for several months. This may cause unexpected problems in a number of areas of your life. The first will be in connection with children because they may behave in an unpredictable manner for a while. The second is in creative pursuits because although you may have some really great ideas, it may be hard for you to put them into practice. The third is in connection with the kind of love affair that one may enter into purely for fun – and we all know the trouble that can lead to!

LIBRA

SUNDAY, 23RD MAY
Mercury into Gemini

Mercury enters your Solar house of intellectual adventure from today and stimulates your curiosity. Everything from international affairs to religious questions will tax your mind. Your desire to travel will be boosted for a few weeks, as indeed will a need to expand your knowledge, perhaps by taking up a course at a local college. Keep an open mind and allow yourself encounters with new ideas.

MONDAY, 24TH MAY
Moon trine Mercury

Things will move quickly today and anything that has been hanging in the air will now come down to earth and get itself sorted out very quickly. If you need to take advice on anything, whether this be an official matter, a visit to an astrologer or simply a chat to a friend, you will be able to find just the right person to help you today. You may take steps to learn something new or to gain some kind of useful skills.

TUESDAY, 25TH MAY
Sun trine Neptune

There is a strange feeling of certainty about everything that you do today; you may feel that your guardian angel is looking after you and directing your every move. You will have the confidence to speak out and say what is on your mind, better still, others will be in the mood to take notice of your opinions. You can make travel plans now if you want to because these too will work out well for you.

WEDNESDAY, 26TH MAY
Sun conjunct Mercury

If you have any kind of legal or official matter to deal with, this would be a good day to get on with it. It is a good time to sign contracts or agreements or to make a business deal. You seem to be taking a deep interest in spiritual matters now and this may be the start of something which will affect the course of your life from here on.

THURSDAY, 27TH MAY
Moon square Neptune

You would love to be able to buy yourself everything your eye lands on but your budget is limited. Never mind, you can still dream of being a millionaire and maybe one day, you could become one!

FRIDAY, 28TH MAY
Mars opposite Jupiter

Before you throw caution to the wind and wildly rejoice at some good news that comes your way, it would be wise to check out the facts first. You may have the wrong end of the stick and you'd only look silly if you allowed your exuberance to get the better of you.

SATURDAY, 29TH MAY
Mars opposite Jupiter

The misguided enthusiasm of a partner will irritate you today. Your other half may be too optimistic for his or her own good, but no matter how hard you try you won't be able to get this across. Arguments are likely as issues get blown out of proportion!

SUNDAY, 30TH MAY
Full Moon

This is likely to be a really awkward day for any kind of travelling that you have to do. A vehicle could let you down just when you most need it or the public transport that you usually rely on could suddenly disappear from the face of the earth.

MONDAY, 31ST MAY
Venus square Mars

There seems to be something or somebody standing in the way of your progress today. However hard you work, trying to impress others with your diligence will be an uphill struggle for a while. This doesn't mean that you shouldn't make the effort; it is just that others will seem to have all the glamour, success and also the accolades that you would like. Fortunately, this trend is only temporary.

June at a Glance

LOVE	❤	❤	❤	❤	
WORK	★	★	★	★	★
MONEY	£	£			
HEALTH	✛	✛	✛		
LUCK	U	U	U	U	U

TUESDAY, 1ST JUNE
Venus square Jupiter

Don't believe expressions of affection and regard that are made to you today, there's an underlying motive lurking around somewhere, and it is likely to be nasty. You'll want to think the best but the evidence indicates that a flatterer doesn't bear you any goodwill.

WEDNESDAY, 2ND JUNE
Sun opposite Pluto

Your recent successes will bring a backlash of jealousy and spite from others and you may be surprised at the direction that this is coming from. Try not to put other people's backs up or to rub their noses in your success, but don't allow them to push you off your chosen path either. Destroying your confidence in yourself may give others a short period of satisfaction, but in the long term it won't give them the stardom that they long for.

THURSDAY, 3RD JUNE
Mars direct

The languid atmosphere recedes as Mars resumes a direct course in your sign today. You'll feel more energetic and vital from now on, though there are downsides too. For instance, your general impatience is set to increase, as are the possibilities of doing yourself some minor harm through cuts or burns. Enjoy the renewed vitality by all means, but don't blame us if you do some damage because you're rushing about.

FRIDAY, 4TH JUNE
Mercury trine Mars

Mind and body are in perfect harmony today. Mercury trines Mars bringing you to a peak of perfection, both physically and mentally. You're raring to go, ready to take on any challenge that the world throws at you. Of course, you will present a rather formidable prospect to people you have to deal with, but your attitude proves that it is their problem. If you can't get answers or results today, then you aren't trying!

SATURDAY, 5TH JUNE
Venus into Leo

Venus moves into your eleventh house of friendship and group activities today, bringing a few weeks of happiness and harmony for you and your friends. You could fall in love under this transit or you could reaffirm your feelings towards a current partner. You should be looking and feeling rather good now but, if not, this is a good time to spend some money on your appearance and to do something about any nagging health problems.

SUNDAY, 6TH JUNE
Moon square Pluto

It may be hard to work out what other people want from you because they aren't behaving in a straightforward manner. The problem may be in connection with people at your place of work or it may arise in a social setting. Wherever and whatever it is, guard against believing all that you hear or of allowing yourself to be manipulated by others.

MONDAY, 7TH JUNE
Mercury into Cancer

There's a certain flexibility entering your career structure as indicated by the presence of Mercury in your Solar area of ambition from today. You can now turn your acute mind to all sorts of career problems and solve them to everyone's satisfaction, and your own personal advantage. Your powers of persuasion will be heightened from now on, ensuring that you charm bosses and employers to get your own way. If you are seeking work you should attend interviews because your personality will shine.

TUESDAY, 8TH JUNE
Sun trine Uranus

This is a good time to travel and also to indulge the more intellectual side of your personality. It is a day to go somewhere new and experience something new to you. You might encounter an unconventional person who will open your eyes to new possibilities.

WEDNESDAY, 9TH JUNE
Moon sextile Uranus

After a phase when your loved ones and your closest friends seem to have been living on a different planet to you, you can now begin to count once again upon their support and understanding. Those of you who are single and lonely, will soon have plenty of opportunities to meet new people and to change your lives for the better. If you are alone and lonely, you could find a real soulmate today.

THURSDAY, 10TH JUNE
Venus opposite Neptune

Dreams and reality seem to be heading for a clash today because you know what you would like your life to be like but you probably cannot achieve these dreams just yet. Maybe in time you will if you keep your eye on the ball long enough. You may want to sit around and think but work must be done and the family must be fed. Shame, isn't it?

FRIDAY, 11TH JUNE
Moon square Uranus

Don't believe all that you hear because it may be exaggerated or twisted in some way. If a friend asks you to lend them money or, more likely, to put money into some daft venture, think hard before you agree. It is always far better to give than to lend, so reduce the amount that they want and give it as an outright gift if you want to. This is not an investment, so don't go looking for any kind of return.

SATURDAY, 12TH JUNE
Moon trine Neptune

Romance seems to be in the air and, if you haven't already fallen in love, you are in big danger of doing so soon. The object of your desires could be a wonderful man or lovely lady from a distant and exotic land. If there is no real live person for you to fall in love with, you may be temporarily taken out of yourself by dreaming about a television or film actor or actress.

SUNDAY, 13TH JUNE
New Moon

The New Moon in your house of adventure urges you to push ahead with new projects. You're in a self-confident mood, and feel able to tackle anything the world throws at you. There's a lure of the exotic today because far-off places will exert a powerful attraction. Think again about widening your personal horizons, by travel or by taking up an educational course. Intellectually you're on top form and your curiosity is boundless.

MONDAY, 14TH JUNE
Venus trine Pluto

Love could come your way from one of the most unexpected places. You may think you are simply trotting out to visit your local shops and pick up a few stamps at the post office, only to meet the love of your life in the supermarket!

TUESDAY, 15TH JUNE
Mercury sextile Saturn

Just when you are getting fed up with being good, working hard and performing all your duties efficiently and without complaint, your lover will phone and propose a lovely evening off, away from all those onerous chores. Great stuff!

LIBRA

WEDNESDAY, 16TH JUNE
Sun trine Mars

The Solar aspect to Mars gives a terrific boost to your energy and zest for life. You long for the wide-open spaces and will be off on a search for adventure at the drop of a hat. This is no time for sticking to the familiar, for the more outgoing and courageous you are, the greater the satisfaction you'll gain.

THURSDAY, 17TH JUNE
Moon opposite Uranus

If you have never felt like kicking over the traces before and doing something completely different, you will feel like that now. You are in a rebellious and angry mood and anything could happen. Your family, friends and especially your children will be amazed and astounded at your outbursts today. This could be no bad thing because you may need to give them all a shock or two.

FRIDAY, 18TH JUNE
Moon trine Jupiter

If you want to meet interesting members of the opposite sex, then get your friends to take you along to their social and club events. Take a friend along to anything new that appears on your social scene and see what transpires. If you are happily settled with your partner, then talk over your future plans and work out what you can and cannot afford in the coming year. Better still, plan a holiday for later in the year.

SATURDAY, 19TH JUNE
Venus square Saturn

Your active enthusiasm is often infectious, but not today. Venus is in harsh aspect to Saturn which puts everyone else in a rather gloomy frame of mind. You seem unaffected by this, but all this pessimism around you will lower your spirits unless you guard against it. You know full well that the financial picture isn't as bad as all that, but convincing anyone of the fact will be an uphill struggle.

SUNDAY, 20TH JUNE
Sun sextile Jupiter

If you and your partner can get away for a break now, this would do you the world of good. Even if you cannot have a full-scale holiday, a night out or a spell of time doing something different from your usual routine would buck you both up. You may get involved with some kind of sporting activity now with a group of friends and some of you will get out into the country with a partner and enjoy a bit of fresh air.

LIBRA

MONDAY, 21ST JUNE
Sun into Cancer

The Sun moves decisively into your horoscope area of ambition from today bringing in an month when your worldly progress will achieve absolute priority. You need to feel that what you are doing is worthwhile and has more meaning than simply paying the bills. You may feel the urge to change your career, to make a long-term commitment to a worthwhile cause, or simply to demand recognition for past efforts. However this ambitious phase manifests itself you can be sure that your prospects are considerably boosted from now on.

TUESDAY, 22ND JUNE
Venus opposite Uranus

It is not going to be the easiest day for either friendships or love affairs. Your desires are not the top priority today and you could find yourself overruled even in the most trivial of matters. Have courage, this influence will not last long.

WEDNESDAY, 23RD JUNE
Mercury square Mars

Whatever you try to say today will seem to come out wrong. You may be so irritated by the behaviour of others that you lose your temper and thus lose your grip on the argument. It will be very hard for you to keep your cool because you want to move quickly and get things done fast today, while others are causing you delays and frustrations.

THURSDAY, 24TH JUNE
Moon opposite Saturn

The Lunar opposition to Saturn shows that this, unfortunately, is one of those days when you can't seem to make any headway at all. Everywhere you turn there are obstacles and delays. Cash affairs are worst hit in this grim outlook and become more complex by the minute. Though you won't want to hear it, patience will solve all problems. Don't lose your temper because that won't help. The worst of the financial troubles should be over by tomorrow.

FRIDAY, 25TH JUNE
Mercury square Jupiter

You will be at cross purposes with everyone around you today. You seem to be trying so hard to achieve a particular ambition, and other people seem to be dragging their feet and making it almost impossible for you to get anywhere. You need new faces around you and new contacts who might have the answers to your problems but it is hard to find the right people just now.

SATURDAY, 26TH JUNE
Mercury into Leo

The swift-moving planet Mercury enters your eleventh Solar house today and gives a remarkable uplift to your social prospects. During the next few weeks you'll find yourself at the centre point of friendly interactions. People will seek you out for the pleasure of your company. It is also a good time to get in contact with distant friends and those you haven't seen for a while. The only fly in the ointment is that you shouldn't expect a small phone bill.

SUNDAY, 27TH JUNE
Moon trine Venus

Drudgery can go hang as far as you're concerned now. The Moon makes a splendid aspect to Venus which puts you in a rather frivolous and very sociable frame of mind. You feel a need to go out and visit friends and indulge in the pleasures of conversation. Go with the flow today, and give in to your desires; they seem innocent enough.

MONDAY, 28TH JUNE
Jupiter into Taurus

A shrewd and perceptive inclination is boosted now as Jupiter enters a very sensitive area of your horoscope and you won't be satisfied with superficial or obvious explanations to anything. This planetary change ushers in a year that will be extremely profitable for you, especially if you can save or invest money.

TUESDAY, 29TH JUNE
Moon trine Saturn

You are developing an attitude of strength and authority and this will stand you in good stead when dealing with officials or business people of all kinds. People will take you seriously today.

WEDNESDAY, 30TH JUNE
Mercury opposite Neptune

You may expect friends to be ready to give you a hand at all times, and most of the time they are. However, today, your pals seem to have other fish to fry and you will simply have to find ways to amuse yourself that don't depend upon the company of others.

July at a Glance

LOVE	❤			
WORK	★	★		
MONEY	£	£	£	
HEALTH	✪	✪	✪	✪
LUCK	U	U	U	

THURSDAY, 1ST JULY
Moon sextile Pluto

A rather pleasant planetary aspect could turn what is already a nice day into a truly spectacular one. You may make a financial killing or you could hear great news from a family member (or both). Love, sex and affection will be high on your agenda, so snuggle up with your loved one on the sofa tonight and let nature take its course in the time-honoured manner.

FRIDAY, 2ND JULY
Moon opposite Venus

Your energy level is low at the moment, so don't set yourself a list of tiresome tasks. Just go through the motions while at work. Plan an evening of resting on the sofa, watching your favourite video or chatting idly to your lover. Don't put any demands upon yourself today, get a take-away dinner (a "carry-out" to all our American readers!) and read the papers until you doze off.

SATURDAY, 3RD JULY
Moon trine Mars

Your energy level is very high today and you will be able to get a great deal done. You will zip through the chores as though someone were chasing you, or as if you were being paid piecework rates! This may be in order to get your hands on some extra money or simply because you are in a particularly productive frame of mind. You may even be working off a certain amount of anger against someone.

SUNDAY, 4TH JULY
Mars opposite Jupiter

Fools rush in where angels fear to tread, and that's exactly what would happen to you if you were to follow your impulses today. In all money matters caution should be your watchword. Take care that you don't bite off more than you can chew with loans, mortgages and overdraughts.

MONDAY, 5TH JULY
Mars into Scorpio

Active, energetic Mars marches into your Solar second house of personal finances today. This should bring you a few weeks of opportunity in connection with money matters. Your attitude will be quite materialistic for a while and you will spend quite a bit of time looking at catalogues, newspapers and shop windows in order to get the best goods your new-found money will be able to provide.

TUESDAY, 6TH JULY
Moon square Sun

Some peace and quiet is the order of the day, that is if you can find some. There are still a lot of demands made upon you but you need some time to yourself, perhaps engaged in a favourite hobby to refresh your spirit. Too much interference from others will only result in you losing your temper. Put up a 'Do Not Disturb' sign, you'll feel better for a little solitude.

WEDNESDAY, 7TH JULY
Moon trine Venus

Things are looking up now! Those of you who are alone and lonely would do well to get out and about today, because there is definitely something in the air. A friend may introduce you to a potential mate or you may make new friends now who may turn into lovers at a later date. Those of you who are happily settled will enjoy the company of your partner and also that of good friends later on today.

THURSDAY, 8TH JULY
Mercury trine Pluto

Originality is your watchword today because you are simply buzzing with great ideas. You can find your way around the most peculiar of problems and come up with ingenious answers to almost anything now.

FRIDAY, 9TH JULY
Moon square Venus

You like to please but that instinct can be taken too far especially if someone you wish to win as a friend is unresponsive or seems to take your attention for granted. You usually know that goodwill can't be bought so why are you taking so much trouble to do just that now? Be aware that someone around you is trying to take advantage of your good nature.

SATURDAY, 10TH JULY
Moon sextile Mercury

You're terribly restless today and can't wait to get away from the jaded and familiar. Though your basic inclinations may be to travel as far away as you can, you'd be the first to admit that it is not always possible. If you are chained to the domestic or work scene, then you need something to take your mind off the usual affairs of your life. A good conversation, a fascinating book or absorbing television show should improve your mood.

SUNDAY, 11TH JULY
Mars square Neptune

Though you strongly desire some fun, you may find that the financial realities won't stand the strain! You'll be particularly self-indulgent now, but some of the treats you have in mind are pricey, so take care!

MONDAY, 12TH JULY
Mercury retrograde

Today begins a period when your optimism will fall short of its usual level. It is the fault of Mercury which turns retrograde. This isn't a serious problem but you must be aware that at times you will feel as if your hopes have been dashed and your faith in friends misplaced. Of course there's little substance in these feelings yet rumours in the next few weeks may be disturbing.

TUESDAY, 13TH JULY
New Moon

The new Moon points to the great heights that you could possibly attain. The message is that there's nothing to fear except fear itself. Reach for the stars and you've got it made. Your career should begin to blossom now and you can achieve the kind of respect and status that you are looking for over the next month or so.

WEDNESDAY, 14TH JULY
Moon conjunct Mercury

It is a good day to get in touch with friends that you haven't seen in ages. Keep some blank spaces in your diary for a few select social events this week. It would be good to talk things over with some special people in your life. Though you're in a thoughtful frame of mind for much of the time it's an excellent idea to get another perspective on your plans.

LIBRA

THURSDAY, 15TH JULY
Venus trine Jupiter

This is a great day for partnership matters of all kinds. Love relationships could take off like a rocket now with both a loving and a very sensual element incorporated in them. Business or other working partnerships will be extremely successful, particularly where money and shared resources are concerned. There is a feeling of karmic benefits coming your way, meaning that good deeds will now be repaid.

FRIDAY, 16TH JULY
Mercury trine Pluto

There's no doubt that you are a persuasive person, especially when you have a bee in your bonnet. Today, you could sway anyone to your cause, and turn opponents into supporters.

SATURDAY, 17TH JULY
Void Moon

The Moon is 'void of course' today, so don't bother with anything important and don't start anything new now. Stick to your usual routines and don't change your lifestyle in any way.

SUNDAY, 18TH JULY
Saturn square Uranus

Some financial problems are going to rear their ugly heads today. Usually you could deal with these in a calm fashion; however, you are too excited to be completely rational at the moment.

MONDAY, 19TH JULY
Moon trine Uranus

This is one of those strange days when almost anything could happen. One of the most likely options is that you could fall deeply and passionately in love! The chances are that any such love affair would be fairly short-lived, on the basis that something that starts with an explosion soon burns itself out.

TUESDAY, 20TH JULY
Moon square Sun

A world-weary mood takes hold under a harsh Lunar aspect to the Sun today. You've put up with a lot of pressures recently, and even though the more general outlook is good, you are showing the strain. The expectations of others create a major problem. You've done a lot for other people over the past few weeks and you could do with a day off.

LIBRA

WEDNESDAY, 21ST JULY
Jupiter square Neptune

The promise of money is likely to be overly optimistic in the extreme today. Keep your tongue in your cheek and don't lend any of your hard-earned. Otherwise you'll be out of pocket.

THURSDAY, 22ND JULY
Mercury square Mars

There's an argumentative atmosphere today. The aggression of Mars unites with the verbal dexterity of Mercury so sarcasm, sniping comments and backbiting could so easily turn into a full-blown quarrel. Everyone seems too nervy for their own good, and that goes for you too. If you want a confrontation, you'll certainly find one, but remember harsh words are easily spoken but it is not so easy to take them back afterwards. Try not to let your temper get the better of you now.

FRIDAY, 23RD JULY
Sun into Leo

As the Sun makes its yearly entrance into your eleventh Solar house, you can be sure that friends and acquaintances are going to have a powerful influence on your prospects. The Sun's harmonious angle to your own sign gives an optimism and vitality to your outgoing nature. Social life will increase in importance over the next month. You'll be a popular and much sought-after person. Obstacles that have irritated you will now be swept away.

SATURDAY, 24TH JULY
Moon sextile Uranus

This is a great day for those of you who are involved with children or young people. If you are a teacher, a scout leader or something similar, you will have a lot of fun and a gratifying level of success in your endeavours today. If you are not involved with youngsters, then be a youngster yourself for once, go bowling, play with your computer or dance around the house to the music on your radio.

SUNDAY, 25TH JULY
Mercury square Jupiter

Try to moderate your expectations today. Though both Mercury and Jupiter encourage some grandiose schemes, they aren't exactly grounded in practicality. Though it is true that you should be ambitious, you can't make castles in the air and then move into them. Don't be too ready to make promises today since you know that you'll be unlikely to keep them.

LIBRA

MONDAY, 26TH JULY
Sun opposite Neptune

If you are in a sentimental and soppy mood today, something or somebody is likely to come along and spoil it for you. You cannot cope with too much reality just now but, unfortunately, reality is just what you will have to get to grips with, whether you like it or not.

TUESDAY, 27TH JULY
Sun square Jupiter

Brimming with confidence, you feel you could take on the world and win today. Never mind the duties already on your agenda, you could so easily take on more because you're convinced that you could handle it all, and still have time for a relaxing drink afterwards. If you follow this overly optimistic course, you'll be a fool to yourself. You can't possibly manage everything on your own, no matter how confident you feel. You'll be making a rod for your own back and piling up the stress levels through overwork if you aren't careful. Be more sensible and set yourself a practical schedule.

WEDNESDAY, 28TH JULY
Full Moon eclipse

Today's eclipse casts a shadow over your sense of fun and frivolity. Life may seem too serious to be bothered with flippant activities or people. A serious attitude will prevail but that shouldn't get you down. Nothing has really changed so your mood should soon lighten up.

THURSDAY, 29TH JULY
Moon square Saturn

You have a yearning for freedom now but that the planets decree a restriction of your freedom for the moment. You may feel that you are entitled to a little recreation, but the call of duty is strong, and the bank balance isn't up to any expensive flights of fancy yet. You must be realistic and balance the call of duty with your need for time to yourself.

FRIDAY, 30TH JULY
Sun trine Pluto

Even if you never thought that you could stand in front of an audience and hold them in the palm of your hand, today's stars could prove you wrong! The excellent aspect between Pluto and the Sun shows you to be a powerful orator capable of swaying the minds and emotions of all who hear you. You should perhaps consider taking it up full time.

SATURDAY, 31ST JULY
Mercury retrograde

A job you had thought was completed could come back with a vengeance today. In many ways you'll feel that you are forced back to square one, yet going over old ground will enable you to spot and put right previous mistakes.

August at a Glance

LOVE	❤				
WORK	★	★			
MONEY	£	£	£	£	£
HEALTH	☉	☉	☉	☉	
LUCK	♘	♘	♘	♘	♘

SUNDAY, 1ST AUGUST
Moon trine Mercury

Don't be afraid to seek out your boss or other authority figure today because as long as you offer sensible suggestions, these will be well received. You will be able to get your point of view across and enhance your professional standing at the same time.

MONDAY, 2ND AUGUST
Moon trine Sun

Personal relationships seem to be uppermost in your mind at the moment and there is a fair chance that you will be happy as a result of this today. You and your lover could enjoy a truly memorable evening out on the town followed by a champagne-soaked love-making session. If you are truly single and all alone today, then you may meet someone who turns your heart and stomach to jelly.

TUESDAY, 3RD AUGUST
Venus trine Jupiter

The excellent aspect between the two planets of good fortune, Venus and Jupiter, boost your prospects in both your financial life and personal affairs. Love isn't far from you now, and whether you're single or emotionally linked this will be a time to get together with someone who understands how you feel and returns your affection.

LIBRA

WEDNESDAY, 4TH AUGUST
Moon trine Venus

Your imagination is very powerful today, and your thoughts will turn to the romantic and erotic issues of your life again and again. It is said that dreams are quite often more fun than fact and that's certainly true of your mood today. This can't be bad for your sex life since your imagination can only provide some spice to your relationship.

THURSDAY, 5TH AUGUST
Moon conjunct Saturn

The subject of money tends to be depressing today. The Lunar conjunction with Saturn puts you in rather a grim frame of mind for much of the time. You have some big ideas but when you consider all the expense and effort required it is not surprising that you feel discouraged. The picture isn't really as bad as all that, remember that every cloud has a silver lining somewhere!

FRIDAY, 6TH AUGUST
Mercury direct

Mercury returns to direct motion from today and that should put a stop to all the setbacks and disappointments that have bedevilled your career for the last few weeks. Suddenly, plans you'd put on the back burner are important again, your path towards your aims will be much smoother than you expect. An ongoing dialogue with an employer or manager will be beneficial to your career prospects.

SATURDAY, 7TH AUGUST
Sun square Mars

This is not going to be a smooth, well-ordered day. The Sun makes a harsh aspect to Mars which sets tempers on edge and reduces patience to zero. If you are involved in a dispute with a friend over money the situation could become intolerable. Friendships are bound to suffer when one or both of you come out with complaints and accusations that can hardly be forgiven. Try to think before you speak. Once the words are out, it'll be too late.

SUNDAY, 8TH AUGUST
Sun opposite Uranus

Take care today because you could injure yourself accidentally. Be especially careful to warm up before doing any kind of sport or exercise and also to cool down again gently before jumping in the car or catching the bus home afterwards. If you do want to exercise today, you would probably be better off doing something gentle such as swimming or taking the dog for a walk.

LIBRA

MONDAY, 9TH AUGUST
Moon sextile Saturn

Financially you'll be a wizard today. You can get your head around the most intractable problem, official form or even deal with officious authorities, and still get what you want. You'll be extremely efficient and capable.

TUESDAY, 10TH AUGUST
Sun square Saturn

Though you have a strong urge for freedom now, the possibilities of escape are limited to say the least. The light of the Sun is dimmed by the cold planet Saturn, and that will make you dissatisfied with your lot. As the day goes on, you'll realize that there's not a lot of point trying to put duties off, or to evade any responsibility. Be as straightforward as possible and you'll find that you can get through a mountain of tasks. Think about the sense of relief you'll feel when it is all over.

WEDNESDAY, 11TH AUGUST
New Moon eclipse

Today's Lunar eclipse may make you feel uncomfortable around people but it is not as bad as Nostradamus's prediction for this day, which includes doom and disaster for all. Assuming he's wrong, the worst you'll get is being painfully aware of your character defects or supposed inferiorities. Nothing could be further from the truth since you come over as a capable and amusing companion. Try to shake off any feelings of negativity. If you truly are concerned while comparing yourself to new acquaintances, remember that they're bound to have faults too.

THURSDAY, 12TH AUGUST
Mercury into Leo

Mercury will soon start to bring a remarkable uplift to your social prospects and your life will be more enjoyable and amusing than for some time past. You can expect a laugh with your friends and a sudden and unexpected invitation to far-flung places. You will enjoy some quiet moments when you can sit down and do some serious thinking.

FRIDAY, 13TH AUGUST
Mercury opposite Neptune

Some of your friends' ideas about fun won't win favour with you today. In fact you may consider the whole pack of them to be nothing more than fools. Hold back on criticisms for now though, or you may regret your words later!

LIBRA

SATURDAY, 14TH AUGUST
Mars opposite Saturn

You could be prone to worry over money today, but the last thing you should do is try to spend your way out of debt. Look at all financial agreements very carefully indeed and make sure that you aren't overburdening yourself unnecessarily.

SUNDAY, 15TH AUGUST
Venus retrograde

Venus pays a return visit to one of the most social areas of your chart today, showing that for a short while you'll have to deal sympathetically with the emotional concerns of a friend. Your capacity for understanding will be enhanced.

MONDAY, 16TH AUGUST
Moon sextile Sun

A fortunate day in which the rays of the Moon and Sun mingle to bring you happy times in the company of friends. It could be that someone around you has had a stroke of luck and wishes to share this good fortune.

TUESDAY, 17TH AUGUST
Mercury square Jupiter

If you can avoid spending money today, then do so because anything that you buy now could turn out to be a dead loss. It isn't worth trying to put ideas into action now either because they could also turn out to be costly mistakes. Try to avoid signing anything important if you can. There may be some kind of legal or official matter to deal with but try not to let this frighten you unnecessarily.

WEDNESDAY, 18TH AUGUST
Moon opposite Saturn

Make sure that you have your credit cards, petty cash and purse in a safe place today, as you're apt to find yourself with less resources than you thought at the worst possible moment. Be cautious and always have a fallback just in case you don't have enough cash on you when it's time to pay the bill. Don't take minor setbacks to heart today. Be prepared!

THURSDAY, 19TH AUGUST
Pluto direct

This is the day when Pluto turns to direct motion. This is, in a way, the end of an era. In your case, there may soon be changes in your family structure, especially in connection with brothers and sisters. You may start to move among a new and rather different circle of people, leaving the old one behind for ever.

LIBRA

FRIDAY, 20TH AUGUST
Sun conjunct Venus

A friendship that has built up in a professional environment will be worth its weight in gold now, since a hint or favour will come your way just because you are liked. Women in the workplace are powerfully placed to help you out, and the goodwill of colleagues and bosses will aid your progress no end. Diplomatically you'll chart a course to high achievement now.

SATURDAY, 21ST AUGUST
Moon trine Venus

It is an excellent day for anyone with an outgoing nature. In fact, it is so good that even the most solitary person will be tempted from a protective shell. Your joy in life is strongly emphasized today. This is no time for worry or moans. Get out and about. Enjoy yourself and you'll find plenty of good companionship along the way.

SUNDAY, 22ND AUGUST
Moon trine Jupiter

This is a great day for making money in or around your home and it is especially fortunate for those of you who run a small business from home. If you don't, then plan a garage sale or offer your services to neighbours and local friends and you will be able to make a small but useful amount of cash.

MONDAY, 23RD AUGUST
Sun into Virgo

The Sun moves into your house of secrets and psychology today making you very aware of your own inner world of dreams and imagination. For the next month you'll be sensitive to the hurdles that face you and things that tend to restrict your freedom. Your imagination and enhanced intuition will provide the necessary clues to overcome these obstacles. Issues of privacy are very important for the next few weeks.

TUESDAY, 24TH AUGUST
Venus square Mars

There's rather a tense atmosphere about you today as the energies of Mars and Venus spread disharmony amongst your friends and associates. You must avoid becoming involved in other people's marital crises, or to take sides in a dispute between friends, but the only way you'll avoid it is by making yourself scarce for a while. If you don't want a dispute of your own, then don't borrow or lend money now.

LIBRA

WEDNESDAY, 25TH AUGUST
Jupiter retrograde

Jupiter goes into retrograde motion from today so finances may go into a temporary dip for a while. Don't despair, even though luck doesn't seem to be on your side at the moment. This could be an opportunity to get your books in order and to root out unnecessary expenses.

THURSDAY, 26TH AUGUST
Full Moon

Something is coming to a head in relation to your job. This is not a major crisis and there is absolutely no need to flounce out of a perfectly good job, but there is a problem that should be solved before you can continue on in a happy and peaceful frame of mind. You may have to sort out what your role is and which part of the job other people should be doing, because it looks as if you are carrying too much of the load at the moment.

FRIDAY, 27TH AUGUST
Mercury conjunct Venus

Influential friends are a help to anybody but today such people will come rushing to your aid. You may be offered an unusual job or given an excellent opportunity to enlarge your experience of life.

SATURDAY, 28TH AUGUST
Sun trine Jupiter

All work affairs receive a welcome boost from the fortunate rays of the Sun and Jupiter today. The prospects for advancement are good, but they really shine if you happen to work for a company with foreign connections. The expansive influence opens many doorways of opportunity. Reach for the sky and you'll achieve great things. Those without work will find that luck is on their side now. Some may seek employment in another country.

SUNDAY, 29TH AUGUST
Moon trine Pluto

Close relationships are moving into a much better phase now. Perhaps you are both learning to listen to each other and to take each other's thinking into account. You could discover that someone whom you considered as nothing more than a friend or a colleague is harbouring deep feelings about you. What you do about this is up to you.

MONDAY, 30TH AUGUST
Saturn retrograde

Saturn turns to retrograde motion today, heralding a difficult phase in connection with money and business matters. You may find that the people and organizations that you routinely deal with are slow in answering important letters and particularly slow in paying for anything.

TUESDAY, 31ST AUGUST
Mercury into Virgo

You'll find yourself in a more introspective mood for a few weeks because Mercury, planet of the mind, enters the most secret and inward-looking portion of your horoscope from today. This is the start of a period when you'll want to understand the inner being, your own desires and motivations. Too much hectic life will prove a distraction now so go by instinct and seek out solitude when you feel like it.

September at a Glance

LOVE	❤	❤	❤	
WORK	★	★	★	★
MONEY	£	£	£	
HEALTH	☉	☉	☉	☉
LUCK	☋			

WEDNESDAY, 1ST SEPTEMBER
Moon square Venus

We all like to be liked, but don't you think that you're taking your desire to please too far? Someone around you is all too prepared to take advantage of your goodwill and seems to grow more demanding by the hour. A friend who is constantly imposing on your good nature may be taking you for a fool. Remember that true friendship is a two-way affair, and can't be bought.

THURSDAY, 2ND SEPTEMBER
Mars into Sagittarius

Mars marches into your communications house today, so direct and forceful speech will be a feature of the next few weeks. If you've got something to say, then there's no power in heaven or earth that's going to prevent you from saying it! If talking to a friend or relative has been like walking on eggshells, you'll make it clear that you aren't going to pussyfoot around sensitive topics any more! Be prepared for some heated words to clear the air!

FRIDAY, 3RD SEPTEMBER
Mercury trine Jupiter

No one had better try to pull the wool over your eyes today. Your perception, swift understanding and lightening reflexes ensure that you could out-talk, out-think and outmanoeuvre all opponents and rivals. In business affairs, luck is on your side. Add to that an ability to make the most out of the opportunities that come your way, as well as pulling a fast one, this day should be a winner.

SATURDAY, 4TH SEPTEMBER
Mercury square Pluto

You may doubt yourself today and something or somebody will cause you to take a second look at some of your ideas. You may inadvertently say the wrong thing to someone and, worse still, they may take offence at this. It is worth remembering that, as long as you didn't mean to be hurtful, any offence taken is really an indication of the other person's insecurity.

SUNDAY, 5TH SEPTEMBER
Moon sextile Saturn

You can make a shrewd financial move today if you play your cards close to your chest and progress slowly and deliberately towards your goal. Investments and pension policies need attention and can be reworked to your eventual profit.

MONDAY, 6TH SEPTEMBER
Mars sextile Neptune

Being swept off your feet is one thing, but when sudden attraction turns into love divine, all loves excelling, you might have problems, especially if you've got other things to do! If you are unattached though, this could be the big one!

TUESDAY, 7TH SEPTEMBER
Moon opposite Uranus

You cannot resist the winds of change that seem to be blowing through your life today. You may have to get used to some kind of new gadget (especially electrical or computer equipment) and you may feel that you are not as competent in this area as you would like to be. Your children may show you up by being quicker at picking up the technique than you are.

LIBRA

WEDNESDAY, 8TH SEPTEMBER
Sun conjunct Mercury

The Sun and Mercury move into close conjunction today which heightens your imagination to the point of pain. It would be too easy to get carried away with an idea and let baseless fears rule your life. You're quite emotional now, so when the light of reason is overwhelmed by your ego, your anxieties come to the fore. Don't be taken in by flights of fancy.

THURSDAY, 9TH SEPTEMBER
New Moon

The world of romance is especially attractive on a day when your dreams and fantasies take over your life. The New Moon points the way to new emotional experiences in the future, but you mustn't cling to the past because of misplaced loyalty or guilt. Some people are leaving your life, but if you were honest you'd admit that they're no real loss. Follow your instincts now and your dreams may well come true.

FRIDAY, 10TH SEPTEMBER
Sun trine Saturn

Any private financial transactions made today should be spelled out in detail to make absolutely sure that you know all there is to know about interest rates and other vital details. Loans taken out now may get you out of trouble, but be arduous to pay back. Today's secret of success lies in clarity. Make sure that you are aware of all the pros and cons in any financial dealing.

SATURDAY, 11TH SEPTEMBER
Venus direct

Venus returns to a more direct path showing that emotional troubles will now be eased. You will find that a friend's heartache will be banished and you can start to think about your own desires and needs.

SUNDAY, 12TH SEPTEMBER
Moon sextile Venus

If you're invited to any social gathering you'd better make up your mind to go, because you'll certainly miss out if you don't attend. If, by some chance, no invitations are forthcoming then invite your friends to a local bar or club. Good company is vital to you now because you need to feel part of a close-knit group for your personality to shine.

LIBRA

MONDAY, 13TH SEPTEMBER
Moon square Neptune

You'll be in the mood to indulge yourself today, whether you can afford it or not. It may only be a little luxury but you know full well that the money you splash out on this could be better spent elsewhere.

TUESDAY, 14TH SEPTEMBER
Moon opposite Saturn

Heavy bills and hefty expenses are the order of the day, because the Moon opposes Saturn making the financial realities of life all too real and rather distressing. It could be time to tighten the belt for a while!

WEDNESDAY, 15TH SEPTEMBER
Mars conjunct Pluto

There could be interesting news in connection with a brother or sister and though this should be good news, it may come as quite a surprise to you. Guard against accidents, especially when driving or even if you have to travel by public transport. Keep your wits about you during this potentially dangerous phase so if you park the car, make sure that any goods that are in it are stowed out of sight and then be sure to lock the car.

THURSDAY, 16TH SEPTEMBER
Mercury into Libra

The movement of Mercury into your own sign signals the start of a period of much clearer thinking for you. You will know where you want to go and what you want to do from now on. It will be quite easy for you to influence others with the brilliance of your ideas and you will also be able to project just the right image. Guard against trying to crowd too much into one day today.

FRIDAY, 17TH SEPTEMBER
Mercury trine Neptune

You will find allies in all the most unexpected places; alternatively, people whom you have helped in the past may come back to help you now. Children and young people may stand up for you, while adults criticize you or let you down. Your creative powers are at quite a high point at the moment, so get started on a relaxing creative hobby if you can.

SATURDAY, 18TH SEPTEMBER
Moon square Mercury

Some piece of domestic machinery that you tend to rely upon could let you down today. This may be something in connection with communications, so expect the radio or the television to go on the blink and your telephone may be out of order for a while. There may be a power cut in your area, possibly due to some kind of freak weather condition.

SUNDAY, 19TH SEPTEMBER
Moon trine Saturn

You'll be in one of those moods when you could take on the world and win today! There is nothing too complex to be handled. No red tape, forms, or documents of any kind will confuse you, and when it comes to money, you're a whizz!

MONDAY, 20TH SEPTEMBER
Moon trine Sun

Be yourself today because there is no need to put on an act for the benefit of others. There shouldn't be anything to stop you being happy at home and also within yourself. You may want to get away from the rat race today and simply relax and do a little pottering about in and around your home. You are in a very creative frame of mind now, so set out to make a cake or design something ingenious if you fancy it.

TUESDAY, 21ST SEPTEMBER
Mercury sextile Pluto

You will be pleased with any news that comes your way now because it could bring the start of a much better time for you regarding business and financial matters. You may hear something interesting from brothers, sisters or neighbours today.

WEDNESDAY, 22ND SEPTEMBER
Moon opposite Venus

Though you may have to give your prospects a kick start, the stellar message is one of creativity and potential. You feel in a particularly artistic mood now, appreciative of painting, music and more cultural pursuits. Unfortunately, both children and friends tend to be quite demanding, so your enlightening idyll will be short-lived or occur in bursts.

THURSDAY, 23RD SEPTEMBER
Sun into Libra

The Sun moves into your own sign today bringing with it a lifting of your spirits and a gaining of confidence all round. Your birthday will soon be here and we hope that it will be a good one for you. You may see more of your family than usual now and there should be some socializing and partying to look forward to. Music belongs to the realm of the Sun, satisfy yourself with a musical treat soon.

FRIDAY, 24TH SEPTEMBER
Mars sextile Uranus

Fast talking and fast thinking are the order of the day as Mars and Uranus shake up your mental state and set you on a course of activity that will take all your powers of observation to deal with. You'll have a razor-sharp mind and superb insight now!

SATURDAY, 25TH SEPTEMBER
Full Moon

The Full Moon shines in the area of close relationships today. Since it is a stress indicator, you'd be wise to build some bridges within a close partnership before you allow an emotional link to drift away. Your understanding and tolerance will be the key to relationship success now.

SUNDAY, 26TH SEPTEMBER
Moon opposite Mercury

'Love don't come easy', as the song says. Well, not today, anyhow. It is not worth trying to get on good terms with your lover, because everything you try to say or do will be misconstrued. Your motives may be the best but your partner will not be in a good mood. He or she may be more interested in having a fit of the sulks than in giving you the love and reassurance that you are searching for.

MONDAY, 27TH SEPTEMBER
Moon square Neptune

Other people may land you with one or two practical problems today, especially concerning joint financial matters. However, you would rather be thinking up ways of having a good time so perhaps you won't even notice the problems.

TUESDAY, 28TH SEPTEMBER
Moon conjunct Saturn

A partner's apparent indifference is only an indication that he has a lot on his mind. Financial worries could be putting a damper on physical expressions of love. Don't take this so much to heart because once the anxiety is over your relationship will soon get back on an even keel. You may feel lonely now, but keep yourself busy, the mood won't last long.

WEDNESDAY, 29TH SEPTEMBER
Moon trine Neptune

If you have your heart set on finding love and romance, today's excellent aspect between the Moon and Neptune makes it easy for you to make your dreams come true. If you long to be the life and soul of the party, today should be your turn to shine.

THURSDAY, 30TH SEPTEMBER
Moon trine Uranus

There should be a number of pleasant surprises today and these will come from distant or unexpected places. You may be invited to join others on a trip overseas or, alternatively, be asked to go out to an interesting and unusual event. It is not worth trying to plan your day because life is likely to be unpredictable.

October at a Glance

LOVE	❤				
WORK	★	★			
MONEY	£	£	£		
HEALTH	✛	✛			
LUCK	♘	♘	♘	♘	♘

FRIDAY, 1ST OCTOBER
Sun sextile Pluto

Though you tend to hate conflict, sometimes a struggle is necessary to crystallize your ideas. There may be an argument today but you can learn a lot about self-presentation and logical debate. You'll win this one because you'll have an ace up your sleeve.

SATURDAY, 2ND OCTOBER
Mercury sextile Venus

Friendships deepen today and new alliances will be made. You may recognize that you feel much more for a friend than you had first realized or that he or she can no longer live without your whole-hearted love and affection. If you need help and advice, then ask yet another good friend today. This is a good time to join groups or to take up a course of study of any kind.

SUNDAY, 3RD OCTOBER
Moon square Mercury

The pressures of life are sometimes too much even for you to bear. Your thoughts are clouded by the Moon and Mercury now so you're in need of an ego boost to offset the criticism and lack of appreciation you've found recently in the workplace. We all need our dreams, so indulge yourself in something you really like, and never mind what anyone else thinks of it.

MONDAY, 4TH OCTOBER
Moon sextile Sun

This should be a day that is notable for fun and a lack of seriousness. The Lunar aspect to the Sun means that your friends take the lead and, if you are willing to follow, they will show you how to have a good time.

TUESDAY, 5TH OCTOBER
Mercury into Scorpio

All the planets seem to be restless at the moment due to Mercury's change of sign today. At least you can get your mind into gear concerning the state of your finances. Tasks such as cancelling useless standing orders, or ensuring you receive the best interest from your savings, will be tackled with ease.

WEDNESDAY, 6TH OCTOBER
Sun trine Uranus

News about any children and young people who may be in your circle will take you by surprise now, but the blessing is that the news will be good. You may discover that your children see you as a friend or they may start to act in a more friendly and co-operative manner from now on. Children could be instrumental in introducing you to a new club, society or a new group of friends now.

THURSDAY, 7TH OCTOBER
Venus into Virgo

As Venus enters your Solar house of secrets and psychology, it is obvious that the next few weeks will increase the importance of discretion in your romantic life. You'll find that it will be wise to draw a veil over the more intimate side of your nature, and you'll be less inclined to confide your deepest secrets even to your closest friends. Quiet interludes with the one you love will be far more attractive than painting the town red just now.

FRIDAY, 8TH OCTOBER
Moon trine Neptune

If there ever was a day in which to please yourself then this is it! Don't burden yourself with duties, in fact if it is at all possible take the day off. The outlook is good for leisure activities, hobbies and a possible romance.

SATURDAY, 9TH OCTOBER
New Moon

There's a New Moon in your own sign. This is a powerfully positive influence that encourages you to make a new start. Personal opportunities are about to change your life. You must now be prepared to leave the past behind to embark on a brand new course. Decide what you want because you'll be your own best guide.

SUNDAY, 10TH OCTOBER
Venus trine Jupiter

You are open to suggestion today, but for once this is no bad thing. The planets Venus and Jupiter ensure that any advice you receive will be to your maximum long-term benefit. This is an excellent outlook for both your savings and all romantic affairs.

MONDAY, 11TH OCTOBER
Jupiter square Neptune

You may have to curb your leisure spending at the moment, even though you will resent this mightily. Jupiter and Neptune present you with few alternatives today so tighten your belt with good grace.

TUESDAY, 12TH OCTOBER
Void Moon

This is not a great day in which to decide anything or to start anything new. A void Moon suggests that there are no major planetary aspects being made, either between planets or involving the Sun or the Moon. This is a fairly unusual situation but it does happen from time to time and the only way to deal with it is to stick to your usual routines and do nothing special for a while.

WEDNESDAY, 13TH OCTOBER
Mercury square Uranus

It will be hard for you to get your act together today. Your ideas are excellent but it may be difficult to get these across to anybody else. Whatever you try to do today will be fraught with constant interruptions and some fairly unreasonable demands upon your time and attention.

LIBRA

THURSDAY, 14TH OCTOBER
Neptune direct

That distant and slow-moving planet, Neptune, turns to direct motion today, ending a rather confusing period in connection with love and sexuality. You may have fallen in love recently, only to find that the object of your desires is only human after all, and that you will have to adapt more to the needs and demands of your lover more than you had previously considered.

FRIDAY, 15TH OCTOBER
Moon conjunct Mars

There could be some interesting events in connection with brothers and sisters today. They may spring a pleasant surprise on you or they may have good news of their own to impart. Neighbours could have cheery things to tell you and all these characters will be very helpful to you if you need them to give you a hand. Any mechanical problems that have been bothering you will be easily solved today.

SATURDAY, 16TH OCTOBER
Mercury opposite Saturn

An opposition between Mercury, the planet of easy communication, and Saturn, the planet of limitations, will make it difficult for you to get your point of view across today. Our guess is that money will be at the heart of this because, although you know what needs to be done, others will be reluctant to hear what you have to say.

SUNDAY, 17TH OCTOBER
Mars into Capricorn

Your energies will be directed to your home and the area around it. Thus you may spend time working on or in the home or on the land around the place today. If the dishes are piling up in the kitchen, then get down to washing them up and if you haven't a clean shirt or a pair of socks to match, then get around to doing the washing now. Mars in the domestic area of your life over the next few weeks could bring a rash of plumbers, builders and all kinds of other domestic workmen your way.

MONDAY, 18TH OCTOBER
Venus square Pluto

Plans are set to be disrupted today, and there's going to be very little that you can do about it. Someone behind the scenes may be working against your interests and you'll have to do some serious digging to find out who this is.

LIBRA

TUESDAY, 19TH OCTOBER
Moon square Saturn

Your mood is on the gloomy side today and the root cause of this is likely to be money. A cash-flow problem could arise, which though temporary, will still be very irritating. Try to look on the bright side.

WEDNESDAY, 20TH OCTOBER
Moon sextile Jupiter

The Lunar aspect to Jupiter shows that this is a lucky day. If you've had any nagging ailments, your symptoms should ease as your general state of health improves. Stress levels should be reduced as your work worries are lessened.

THURSDAY, 21ST OCTOBER
Moon opposite Venus

If your approach to health care involves lots of tasty treats and a somnolent spell stretched out on the sofa, that's all very well, but you know your body needs a spot more physical exercise and discipline to keep it in tip-top shape. Dietary indulgence is your particular bugbear, and today you need to be more than usually vigilant or you'll find your hand in that biscuit tin before you realize it!

FRIDAY, 22ND OCTOBER
Sun square Neptune

All you want to do is to sit and dream but, time, tide, people and life itself won't allow you to. You may feel like behaving in a completely irresponsible manner but you can't. At least get the chores done first and then get out your paints or spend an hour or two tinkling on the piano. When all is quiet and tranquil, get out your old photos or a good novel and sit down in a chair to dream an hour or two away.

SATURDAY, 23RD OCTOBER
Sun into Scorpio

Your financial prospects take an upturn from today as the Sun enters your house of money and possessions. The next month should see an improvement in your economic security. It may be that you need to lay plans to ensure maximum profit now. Don't expect any swift returns from investments but lay down a pattern for future growth and sensible monetary decisions made now will pay off in a big way.

LIBRA

SUNDAY, 24TH OCTOBER
Full Moon

The Full Moon brings to the surface intense feelings that you have buried away in some vault of memory. You'll be forced to look at yourself stripped bare of illusions now. That's not such a bad thing because you'll realize that many of your hang-ups have been a total waste of time and should be ditched. You may have a financial worry coming to a head so today's Full Moon encourages you to take decisive action to sort it out once and for all.

MONDAY, 25TH OCTOBER
Venus trine Saturn

There could be no better time for words of love to be exchanged in private than today… or should we say this evening? The combination of Saturn and Venus may indicate a deepening of emotional commitment and the flowering of long-suppressed passion.

TUESDAY, 26TH OCTOBER
Moon opposite Mercury

You are full of bright and stunning ideas today but we hope that you take your lover's ideas into consideration too. Your capacity for tact is at an all-time low because you can be too truthful for comfort sometimes. Today's Lunar opposition to Mercury could put others' backs up simply because you are too candid. Remember to write down your ideas because they're so good you shouldn't waste any of them.

WEDNESDAY, 27TH OCTOBER
Moon opposite Pluto

Travelling could be a bit awkward today, so if you want to have the best of the day, stay close to home and enjoy being with your family in and around your own house, garden, farm or whatever. If you do need to take a journey, then leave plenty of time for this and expect delays. You may also find it hard to get hold of people on the phone or by fax.

THURSDAY, 28TH OCTOBER
Mercury sextile Neptune

You have the power to turn your own dreams into reality today. If you have some creative idea that you want to develop, this should be easy. If you need to find some specific information in connection with a creative project, you should be able to put your hands on this.

LIBRA

FRIDAY, 29TH OCTOBER
Moon opposite Mars

In all financial dealings it would be well if you let caution be your watchword. The Lunar opposition to Mars will incline you to be rather free with your cash, whether you've got any or not! If you aren't careful, you'll end up providing treats for everyone around you, with no hope of reward.

SATURDAY, 30TH OCTOBER
Mercury into Sagittarius

Your mind will be going at full speed ahead over the next few weeks and you are bound to come up with some really great new ideas. You will be very busy with the phone ringing off its hook and letters falling into your letter box by the ton. You will find yourself acting as a temporary secretary for a while, even if the only person who makes use of your services is yourself.

SUNDAY, 31ST OCTOBER
Moon square Sun

You may decide to treat a friend to a meal out or to a small luxury of some kind. This would be a great idea if you could be sure that your friend would appreciate your generosity. Unfortunately, he or she may take this for granted and your efforts will be wasted.

November at a Glance

LOVE	❤	❤	❤	❤	❤
WORK	★	★			
MONEY	£	£	£		
HEALTH	✚	✚			
LUCK	U	U			

MONDAY, 1ST NOVEMBER
Void Moon

Today is one of those odd days when there are no important planetary aspects being made, not even to the Moon. The best way to tackle these kinds of days is to stick to your usual routine and to avoid starting anything new or tackling anything of major importance. If you do decide to do something large today, then it will take longer and be harder to cope with than it would normally.

TUESDAY, 2ND NOVEMBER
Moon square Mercury

Your mind is racing so fast you can't help causing misunderstandings just now. You may also receive some wounding criticism, though you must admit that you're being a touch over-sensitive. If these hurtful words were actually meant to be constructive, then you could do worse than thinking hard about the issues they raise.

WEDNESDAY, 3RD NOVEMBER
Moon trine Saturn

You will find subtle ways of manipulating others and of bringing them around to your own point of view today. If you feel that a particular venture will go well today, you are probably right.

THURSDAY, 4TH NOVEMBER
Moon sextile Mercury

Being too proud to talk over a problem is a self-defeating attitude. A relative may be in just such a situation and this loved one will need encouragement to open up. All you have to do is listen because the problem could well be solved by simply talking about it. Just smile and nod in the appropriate places and you'll both be all right.

FRIDAY, 5TH NOVEMBER
Moon trine Uranus

You don't seem to be yourself today! Indeed, you seem to be somebody quite different! The problem is that a rather nice aspect between the Moon, which represents habitual behaviour, and Uranus, which represents rebellion, suggests that you will kick over the traces and behave in a completely uncharacteristic manner now.

SATURDAY, 6TH NOVEMBER
Sun opposite Saturn

The Sun opposes Saturn today and reminds you of how far you've actually got to go to achieve your dreams. Financially, a sober outlook will prevail and you'll tend to think that you'll never manage to get enough cash to live the life that you desire. Of course, this is the nature of Saturn, to make reality painfully obvious, but also to look on the black side. If you were truly realistic, you'd see that the picture isn't that bad, and with hard work and dedication you will eventually attain the economic security you crave.

LIBRA

SUNDAY, 7TH NOVEMBER
Sun sextile Mars

Your mood is quite optimistic just now and you seem to have the energy to get the things that you want. Today's aspect is very favourable for anything to do with premises or property so if you want to improve your living place, you can now set about doing this. Your family seem to be in a happy and helpful frame of mind and your lover is in a loving mood too.

MONDAY, 8TH NOVEMBER
New Moon

Today's New Moon shows that your financial affairs have reached a point where you have to make a decision. Do you carry on in the old rather dreary ways of making and spending your cash, or will you look at the realities and make sensible decisions? This isn't a time to retreat into dreamland, or to carry on with bad budgeting so look at your monetary state carefully now.

TUESDAY, 9TH NOVEMBER
Mercury into Scorpio

Mercury's timely entry into your financial sector should be a great help to your situation. Your mind will now be clear and you can see all issues from a logical standpoint. Now you'll be able to budget sensibly, pay off outstanding debts and generally make sense of your cash flow. The shrewdness that Mercury brings to bear on your economic life will enable you to control income and expenditure.

WEDNESDAY, 10TH NOVEMBER
Moon sextile Uranus

If you've ever considered doing something like creative writing, you should start today. You have the inspiration. You have the capability so why not give it a go? You could surprise yourself.

THURSDAY, 11TH NOVEMBER
Moon trine Jupiter

You and your partner are getting on better in general and you are beginning to reach a good understanding where money matters are concerned. There may be more money coming into the family now or you may simply work out a better way of sharing out what there is. If either of you need a replacement vehicle of some kind, this could be on the way soon.

LIBRA

FRIDAY, 12TH NOVEMBER
Moon square Venus

Whatever gender you are, you will find the most help and the best company from among your female friends and relatives today. You will find it easier to relate to women now and, whether you make time for coffee with your sister or a few drinks in the pub with a dear friend, you'll be thanking your lucky stars that you have such an understanding and congenial pal to chat to.

SATURDAY, 13TH NOVEMBER
Moon conjunct Mars

Something will take you back to revisit your past today. You may bump into an old flame and take time out to talk about times gone by, or you may find yourself back in a part of town that you haven't been near for years. Something may help you to come to terms with old hurts and disappointments once and for all today.

SUNDAY, 14TH NOVEMBER
Saturn square Uranus

Financial constraints will be placed upon you today. An irritating fact, which becomes even more annoying when a child is extra-demanding! The contrary natures of Saturn and Uranus will not give you a peaceful time!

MONDAY, 15TH NOVEMBER
Moon square Saturn

The path of true love is rarely smooth and you're due for a bumpy ride today. The issue that afflicts you and your loved one is money, the root of all evil. An understanding is possible but only with effort, and it will take time!

TUESDAY, 16TH NOVEMBER
Mercury sextile Mars

If you are searching for someone who shares your values and priorities, then today's excellent aspect between Mercury and Mars will help you to find just the right person. This doesn't necessarily mean that you will find the love of your life today, but you may discover a soul-mate or a similar type of person to yourself among working colleagues or in your local neighbourhood.

WEDNESDAY, 17TH NOVEMBER
Venus sextile Pluto

You may decide that this is the time to begin re-inventing yourself because, if there are things that you don't like, you can now set about changing them. Take yourself in hand, lose weight if necessary, and generally improve your lifestyle.

THURSDAY, 18TH NOVEMBER
Moon trine Mercury

There should be great news today, especially in connection with your career. If you are looking for a new job now, you should soon hear just the news you need. There is an upturn in matters related to health and whether it is yourself or some other member of your circle who has been under the weather, the news for the future is really good.

FRIDAY, 19TH NOVEMBER
Moon sextile Neptune

This is likely to be a romantic time with a depth of commitment and understanding developing between yourself and somebody very special. A sensitive person who comes into your orbit now will be very appealing.

SATURDAY, 20TH NOVEMBER
Venus trine Uranus

Love, romance and the fun side of sex is likely to be dominating your thoughts and your life at the moment. This will make it impossible for you to make a sensible assessment of your situation and you may be so overwhelmed with feeling that you begin to think that you are losing your mind. Some of you will be experiencing great joy in your lives for some other reason; perhaps the conception or birth of a child or maybe a wedding in the family.

SUNDAY, 21ST NOVEMBER
Mars square Jupiter

Relationships with others are likely to be tense and irritating today. You may have to speak your piece and say what is on your mind. This problem is most likely to centre around the home and family but there could be pressures coming from other directions too. You may not actually find yourself at odds with others but simply propping them up at what is proving to be a time of difficulty for them.

MONDAY, 22ND NOVEMBER
Sun into Sagittarius

Your curiosity will be massively stimulated from today as the Sun enters the area of learning and communication. Other people's business suddenly becomes your own now. That's not to say that you turn into a busybody overnight, it is just that many will turn to you for some guidance. Affairs in the lives of your brothers, sisters and neighbours have extra importance. Short journeys too are well starred for one month.

LIBRA

TUESDAY, 23RD NOVEMBER
Full Moon

You may have to face the fact that you cannot slope off to distant and romantic shores at the moment. This doesn't mean that you are forever confined to your home, just that you cannot get away right now. Your mood is not only escapist but also rebellious today! You won't want to have anything to do with people who restrict you or who remind you of your chores and duties but you simply won't be able to escape them.

WEDNESDAY, 24TH NOVEMBER
Moon trine Venus

You could have a rather nice day in company with in-laws or some other relative of your partner's today. A woman who is vaguely attached to you in this kind of way will turn out to be amusing and interesting company. This person could help you work out how best to go about decorating or changing part of your home or, if you need some help from an experienced cook, she could be the one to come up with the right recipe.

THURSDAY, 25TH NOVEMBER
Sun sextile Neptune

You may become involved in a creative endeavour today or, alternatively, you may find your mind wandering into an area of dreams and fantasy. This does not necessarily mean that you will get drunk or that you will spend a few hours attached to the working end of an opium pipe but you may be involved in local amateur dramatics or something else that is a bit different.

FRIDAY, 26TH NOVEMBER
Mars into Aquarius

Mars moves into a very creative area of your chart now, so if there is a project that you would like to get started upon, Mars will give you the drive and energy with which to do it. This is a good day for any kind of sporting or energetic pursuit so if you want to practise your skills or get ready for some kind of future competition, then get down to it today.

SATURDAY, 27TH NOVEMBER
Moon opposite Neptune

Your feelings could be pretty confused today and you won't be sure of what you actually want. At least you aren't being pressured into making sudden decisions so take it easy and give yourself the time to think.

LIBRA

SUNDAY, 28TH NOVEMBER
Moon square Mercury

A friend may tell you something that upsets you today while another friend may do something that costs you money. With friends like these, do you really need enemies? Your mind is not working at its best now so don't agree to anything or do anything that you are unhappy about or unsure. Wait until your judgement is working at full strength once again.

MONDAY, 29TH NOVEMBER
Mars conjunct Neptune

You are bursting with energy and keen to get on with things today but naughty Neptune is causing muddles and misunderstandings all the way round. Children and young people may have something to do with your state of confusion.

TUESDAY, 30TH NOVEMBER
Moon trine Saturn

Though the prospect of sitting down and working out budgets, investment plans and financial strategies may be boring, it is absolutely vital to your future prospects. The stars decree that this is the day to sort out your cashflow.

December at a Glance

LOVE	❤	❤	❤		
WORK	★	★	★	★	
MONEY	£	£	£	£	£
HEALTH	✪	✪	✪	✪	
LUCK	∪	∪	∪	∪	

WEDNESDAY, 1ST DECEMBER
Venus opposite Jupiter

Affairs of the heart are called into question today as it becomes increasingly obvious that a rift is developing within a relationship. There's little you can do about this at the moment but bear it in mind for the future. Those who are unattached may fall for a glamorous person who has little substance.

LIBRA

THURSDAY, 2ND DECEMBER
Moon sextile Sun

This is a harmonious time when you can express the inner you and find warmth and understanding from those around you. You are charming and persuasive and will be showing your character off to the best advantage.

FRIDAY, 3RD DECEMBER
Moon opposite Jupiter

Other people are not going to see eye to eye with you over money matters today. You and your partner may disagree about how your money is spent (or saved) or you may find yourself at odds with a working partner of some kind. Keep a sense of proportion here and keep hold of your own cash. Don't lend money to others for get-rich-quick schemes and don't allow others to dictate to you about your own spending patterns. Listen to common sense and then make your own mind up about this.

SATURDAY, 4TH DECEMBER
Moon square Neptune

The bank balance may go through a period of temporary emptiness today, which is not to your taste at all. You want to be out painting the town red, but if the money isn't there, you shouldn't push the social boat out too far.

SUNDAY, 5TH DECEMBER
Venus into Scorpio

Your financial state should experience a welcome boost for a few weeks as Venus, one of the planetary indicators of wealth, moves into your Solar house of possessions and economic security from today. You feel that you deserve a lifestyle full of luxury now and that will be reflected in the good taste you express when making purchases for your home. Your sense of self-worth is boosted too which might indicate a renewed interest in high fashion.

MONDAY, 6TH DECEMBER
Sun sextile Uranus

If you are waiting to hear from someone you love, then today should be your lucky day and if money or business has been an obstacle in the path of true love, then the news about this is good too. You may receive a windfall or get some other kind of lucky break and something pleasant but quite unexpected could come your way today.

LIBRA

TUESDAY, 7TH DECEMBER
New Moon

The New Moon shows a change in your way of thinking. In many ways you will know that it is time to move on. Perhaps you'll find yourself in a new company, a new home or among a new circle of friends in the near future. Opinions are set to change as you are influenced by more stimulating people. Perhaps you'll consider taking up an educational course of some kind.

WEDNESDAY, 8TH DECEMBER
Venus square Neptune

The path of true love never did run smoothly and today this will be proved to be so. You may have all kinds of plans for meeting your lover later in the day, only to find that he or she has other ideas.

THURSDAY, 9TH DECEMBER
Moon sextile Venus

There are good vibes surrounding your home, family and personal security today. The Moon is in good aspect to Venus showing good fortune is showered on you and yours. Female relatives can expect excellent news.

FRIDAY, 10TH DECEMBER
Mars square Saturn

Difficult emotional relations could make you very edgy today. Your temper is simmering away and it would only take one minor event for your fury to boil over. Try to take things more calmly.

SATURDAY, 11TH DECEMBER
Mercury into Sagittarius

Your life is going to be extremely busy for a while now and there will be little time to sit around and rest. You will have more to do with friends, relatives, colleagues and neighbours than is usual and you could spend quite a bit of time sorting out minor domestic and work problems with workmen and women of various kinds. You may also spend time and money sorting out a vehicle.

SUNDAY, 12TH DECEMBER
Mercury sextile Neptune

Mercury's wit and wisdom are imparted to you today making all dealings with children that much easier. You can get your message across with no difficulty at all. What's more, your youthful audience will take it all in.

LIBRA

MONDAY, 13TH DECEMBER
Moon sextile Sun

It is a day for simple pleasures and innocent enjoyment. A quiet conversation with a child or younger person should show you that you can still learn a thing or two and have a laugh as well.

TUESDAY, 14TH DECEMBER
Mars conjunct Uranus

It is looks like a day full of passionate intensity as the volcanic influences of Mars and Uranus mingle in your house of romance! Literally anything could happen now and the likelihood is that you'll love every minute and every surprise that comes your way!

WEDNESDAY, 15TH DECEMBER
Venus opposite Saturn

There will be signs of light at the end of the financial tunnel today, but you may have to convince a bank manager or other consultant that this is the case. Patience is definitely a virtue where cash is concerned.

THURSDAY, 16TH DECEMBER
Moon sextile Neptune

This is likely to be an extremely romantic day. The soft rays of the Moon and Neptune put you and someone special in a loving mood. Gentle harmony prevails in all relationships and peace is all around you. Nice change, isn't it?

FRIDAY, 17TH DECEMBER
Sun trine Jupiter

This is a day of good fortune both in professional life and in more personal affairs. You will experience a harmony of purpose and good fortune arising from your partnerships, whether they be of a business nature or on the more emotional side. Any journeys undertaken with someone special will be extremely enjoyable.

SATURDAY, 18TH DECEMBER
Mercury conjunct Pluto

Anything that pops through your letterbox today should bring the kind of news that you most want to hear. Negotiations of all kinds will go well now and it will be easy to turn all situations to your advantage.

LIBRA

SUNDAY, 19TH DECEMBER
Moon conjunct Saturn

The importance of self-love is equally as vital as loving someone else. That's what you're learning now as the Moon conjuncts Saturn in one of the most psychologically sensitive areas of your chart. When you realize your own true worth, it is so much easier to understand the value others place upon you.

MONDAY, 20TH DECEMBER
Jupiter into Aries

A co-operative phase in your life begins today, as Jupiter moves into your house of partnerships for a year-long stay. Teamwork is the key to success, both in personal affairs and in business. Financially, you will benefit from close associations with others as well as learning a thing or two.

TUESDAY, 21ST DECEMBER
Moon opposite Pluto

Guard against being manipulated by others in a way that is against your own interests but, on the other hand, be ready to make adjustments to your own thinking. We can all become ossified, stuck in a rut or simply out-of-date, and then we need to analyse our philosophy of life and see if it is still appropriate. The old ideas of honest, decency and fair-dealing will always be fashionable but some of the details seem to be changing now.

WEDNESDAY, 22ND DECEMBER
Sun into Capricorn

The home and family become your main interest over the next four weeks as the Sun moves into the most domestic area of your chart from today. Family feuds will now be resolved, and you'll find an increasing contentment in your own surroundings. A haven of peace will be restored in your home. This should also be a period of nostalgia when happy memories come flooding back.

THURSDAY, 23RD DECEMBER
Full Moon

There is some evidence of pressure on both your domestic circumstances and also your career situation. This situation has probably been building up for some time, but today a minor event may be just the thing to take the lid off the matter and expose the problems for all to see. Your heart and your feelings are ruling your head, so try to stop and think before speaking.

LIBRA

FRIDAY, 24TH DECEMBER
Venus square Mars

They say that a woman's place is in the wrong! Well, today your place is in the wrong, whatever your gender. You won't be able to please anybody, so try pleasing yourself; at least this way somebody will be satisfied! You may find that other people cost you money or that they take up your time on wild-goose chases or in some other way waste your resources. Younger members of the family will be in a touchy mood too. Sounds like pre-Christmas tension to us!

SATURDAY, 25TH DECEMBER
Moon trine Pluto

You should be able to sort out any power struggles that have been going on around you recently. Your friends or your neighbours may have been playing one off against the other and causing you a good deal of irritation as a result. Try and encourage some of the Christmas spirit. It is supposed to be goodwill to all men, and women too!

SUNDAY, 26TH DECEMBER
Mercury sextile Mars

You may visit family members today or you may be on the receiving end of visits from relatives. Sisters, brothers and grown children may drop in on you, so make sure that you have some extra food in stock, just in case. There could be good news in connection with relatives or possibly related to a business matter that is in hand just now.

MONDAY, 27TH DECEMBER
Mercury trine Jupiter

A stroke of luck is about to strike your partner in life. This is as much good news for you as for the other person involved. Who knows, it might even be you who delivers the glad tidings!

TUESDAY, 28TH DECEMBER
Moon square Mercury

Tactlessness is a trait that has to be watched today. It is too easy to open your mouth and put your foot right in it now and then realize too late what you've said! Your deeper mind is affecting your speech, and though you are coming out with the truth, you could pick a better moment.

LIBRA

WEDNESDAY, 29TH DECEMBER
Moon square Sun

Times of peace and harmony don't last long as you find out today when the tempers are frayed and some family members seem determined to wreck whatever tranquillity remains. You'll feel that all around you are self-seeking and cantankerous. All you want is a quiet life, but you'll have to spend a lot of the day smoothing ruffled feathers. It is only a matter of time before you snap and speak your mind with no room for misunderstanding!

THURSDAY, 30TH DECEMBER
Mars sextile Jupiter

This is quite a lucky day, so try a little wager or two now. Don't put your shirt on anything but have a small gamble on a lottery or a raffle if you get the opportunity. This is also a great time for sporting interests, so whether you are a participant or simply an observer, enjoy your sports today.

FRIDAY, 31ST DECEMBER
Venus into Sagittarius

If you've got any favours to ask, the last day of the year gives you the perfect opportunity. You can use considerable charm and eloquence to win others over to your point of view with no trouble at all. A little flirtation combined with a winning way ensures that you achieve your desires. Your creative talents are boosted too so perhaps you should consider writing down your inspirations now. Happy New Century!